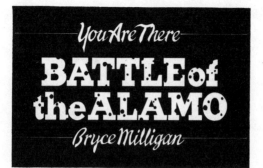

You Are There

BATTLE of
the ALAMO

Bryce Milligan

For Taylor,

Dangerous choices here—
Choose well!

Bryce Milligan

May 1990

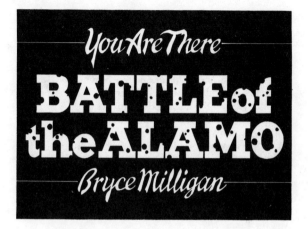

You Are There

BATTLE of the ALAMO

Bryce Milligan

★

TexasMonthlyPress

All illustrations by Charles Shaw

Texas Monthly Press
Post Office Box 1569
Austin, Texas 78767

A   B   C   D   E   F   G

Milligan, Bryce, 1953–
    Battle of the Alamo : you are there / by Bryce Milligan ; illustrated by Charles Shaw.
        p.   cm.
    Summary: As a fourteen-year-old boy involved in the Texas Revolution, the reader makes decisions determining how the story leads up to the Battle of the Alamo.
    ISBN 0-87719-156-5 : $3.95
    1. Alamo (San Antonio, Tex.)–Siege, 1836–Juvenile fiction. 2. Texas–History–To 1846–Juvenile fiction. 3. Plot-your-own stories. [1. Alamo (San Antonio, Tex.)–Siege, 1836–Fiction. 2. Texas–History–To 1846–Fiction. 3. Plot-your-own stories.]
    I. Shaw, Charles, 1941–   ill. II. Title.
P77.M63932Bat   1990
[Fic]–dc20   90-30870
                                                 CIP
                                                  AC

For Michael

ACKNOWLEDGMENTS

My thanks go first to my wife, Mary, who originally encouraged me in this project and then had to put up with its frustrations. Thanks go to Ms. Jo Myler, San Antonio Public Library, History Department, for her speed and accuracy in fielding spur-of-the-moment confirmations of fact on the telephone, as well as for her unerring advice on untried sources. Thanks also to Mary Ann Noonan-Guerra, historian and author, for constant encouragement and for reading the manuscript of this book and others. Finally, thanks to Margaret Cousins, whose children's novel *The Boy in the Alamo* first inspired my interest in Texas history.

INTRODUCTION

You are about to relive one of the most exciting six-month periods in the history of North America. Every event in which you will participate actually happened. The only fictional element is that you are there. You will begin by joining one of the two companies of the New Orleans Greys, which left New Orleans in October 1835 to fight in the Texas Revolution. You will have the opportunity to take part in many of the great events of that war, but whether or not you survive will depend upon your courage and your skills as a frontier fighter. Throughout the story, you will be asked to make decisions based upon your commitment to the ideal of liberty, your own judgement of the situations in which you find yourself, and your knowledge of Texas history. Will you be ambushed along the way? Will you survive the Siege of Béxar during the bitter cold of December 1835? Will you die defending the Alamo or escape unseen? Will you escape the massacre at Goliad or die in front of a Mexican firing squad? Will you live to fight at the final Battle of San Jacinto? Only you can determine your fate. Turn the page and learn something of the chronology of this period. Read it carefully—it could save your life.

CRITICAL INFORMATION

October 2, 1835: Battle of Gonzales (The "Come and Take It" Fight) opens the Texas Revolution

October 9, 1835: Mexican garrison driven out of the Presidio la Bahía at Goliad

October 17, 1835: Departure of the First Company of New Orleans Greys on the Mississippi steamboat *Washita*

October 19, 1835: Departure of the Second Company of New Orleans Greys on the schooner *Columbus*

October 28, 1835: Battle of Concepción, San Antonio. Stephen F. Austin and the Texas army begin the Siege of Béxar

December 5, 1835: The Siege of Béxar culminates in the Texas assault on San Antonio

December 10, 1835: Mexican General Cós surrenders San Antonio de Béxar to the Texans

December 30, 1835: Dr. James Grant and Colonel Johnson depart San Antonio with 200 men to attack Matamoros, Mexico

January 5, 1836: Davy Crockett arrives in Nacogdoches on his way to San Antonio

January 22, 1836: Mexican General Urrea occupies Matamoros; Santa Anna is observed marching north with several thousand troops

February 3, 1836: William Barret Travis arrives at the Alamo

February 8, 1836: Davy Crockett arrives at the Alamo

February 21, 1836: General Santa Anna arrives at the Medina River

February 23, 1836: General Santa Anna enters San Antonio de Béxar

February 24, 1836: Siege of the Alamo begins

February 27, 1836: Most of the Matamoros expedition wiped out at San Patricio and, two days later, at Agua Dulce

March 6, 1836: The Alamo falls

March 13, 1836: Houston leads the army out of Gonzales

March 19, 1836: Battle of Coleto Creek; Fannin surrenders

March 27, 1836: Survivors of Coleto Creek executed at Goliad

April 21, 1836: Battle of San Jacinto

Your name is Thomas Benton. You
are 14 years old.
It is October 1835

You are an Arkansas farm boy. The fifth of five sons, you help work your father's small farm between the Saline and Ouachita rivers in the Ozark Mountains. Your father doesn't believe in slavery, but then he doesn't need to—he has five sons. All your life you have looked at the clear waters of the Ouachita, knowing that they run down to the Red River and then into the great Mississippi and adventure. Robert, your next oldest brother, must have said a thousand times that he would like to take his canoe and head down the river for New Orleans. Then he fell in love and got married. Shoot, he is only 15.

Just after the wedding, he takes you aside to give you some advice. "Look here, Squirt," he says, "I'm stuck in these hills for good now. Don't you do the same. Get in my canoe tonight and head for New Orleans." He gives you his long dirk knife and four dollars in coins. New Orleans, Robert tells you, is the most wonderful place in the world. You figure it is just one stop on the way to the *real* frontier—Texas.

It takes you three full days to make your way down the wandering Ouachita to the Red River. Following the current of the Red, you keep to the middle of the river for another three days and nights. You dare not stop because the banks are infested with alligators where the river passes between dense forests for mile upon mile. You stop only when you come to rocky bluffs where some friendly Cherokees have set up camp. The Indians know a little English and are impressed when you answer them with the few words of Cherokee you learned from the Indians who sometimes came to trade with your father. They invite you to share their meal. As friendly as they seem, you are not sure whether you will have a canoe when you wake up, but you are so tired that there is no choice in the matter. When you do wake up some ten hours later, both your canoe and the Cherokees are still there. You thank them and take to the river again.

A few more days on the Red brings you to the Mississippi, almost a mile wide at this point. Drifting down this great river highway, you cross over to the eastern side—finally, two weeks after running away from the farm, you see the lights of New Orleans just after sundown one October evening. You've never seen so many lights. The docks seem to be strung with one long line of lanterns, and a big riverboat nearby is lit up inside and out, casting bright reflections that shimmer and glitter on the waves.

You have no trouble in selling the canoe

to a man on the riverfront for three dollars, making you fairly well off for the time being. Still, it isn't enough to buy a rifle, which you will need if you want to survive once you get to Texas. Besides, you will need money for the trip, not to mention for staying alive in New Orleans for a few days. So you go looking for a job. At a place called Bank's Arcade, they hire you to wait tables.

New Orleans—where the wild west and the civilized east meet—is a very exciting place. On every street corner you can see traders and trappers, hunters and half-Indians. They wear an assortment of buckskin clothing, generally hung with fringe and often slick with bear grease. At all hours and on every street there are sailors, soldiers, river rats, and gentlemen. Solemn priests and loud street preachers, ladies with dresses five feet wide and men with stovepipe beaver hats a foot tall—since you arrived in New Orleans from upriver two weeks ago, not a day has passed without seeing some new and outlandish character. All the men are armed. The frontier folk carry their long rifles in the crook of their arms and have large knives protruding from their boots, stuck in their belts or hung in sheaths around their necks. Some have tomahawks as well. The men in city

10

clothes or in military uniforms (a dozen different kinds) all have a pistol or two stuck in their belts, and many are armed with swords or Bowie knives.

Turn to page 21

Since you just came down the Red and the Mississippi rivers in a canoe, the idea of retracing the same route, even on a riverboat, just does not appeal to you. Maybe it is the memory of all those alligators. Pushing your way through the crowd of men to the table, you put your name down on the paper marked *Columbus*—the name of the schooner that will take you across the Gulf of Mexico. The man at the table tells you to report to the ship in the morning.

Early the next morning, you are at the dock where the skipper of the *Columbus*, Captain Leidsdorf, is checking off names with his first mate. The *Columbus* itself is anchored in mid-river. Even though you are big for 14, you worry that they will not let you board the ship if they know your real age. But the ship's captain is not in charge of the volunteers; he is just in charge of getting them to Texas. Your age is of no consequence to him. The first mate gives you a scrap of paper with the name of a clothier on it.

"We won't be sailing until the nineteenth," he tells you. "Meantime, you're to get outfitted with a uniform of some sort at this clothier."

Looking you over doubtfully, he adds, "When you report to the *Columbus*, you're to bring a rifle and 100 rounds of ammunition—that's what General Houston wants, and no one is shipping out without them."

You should have gone with Sterne, you think. You do not have enough money to buy a gun *and* a uniform. You head back to the Bank's Arcade to think it over.

Mr. Christy, the man who organized last night's meeting, is just going into the Arcade when you arrive. He is a regular customer of the place, and he asks you, "Well, Tom, did we run you ragged last night? You're looking pretty down in the mouth this morning."

You explain that it is not working so hard last night that has you down, but the fact that you cannot afford both a rifle and a uniform.

"What! Did you sign up to go fight in Texas?" he asks. "Aren't you a bit young for that?"

"I'm as old as my grandfather was when he fought with Gen'l Washington," you tell him. It gives you a good feeling inside to say it. Freeing Texas from the dictator Santa Anna is not so different from freeing the American colonies from King George. " 'Sides," you add, "I came all the way here in a dugout canoe from Arkansas by myself, mainly with an eye to going over to

Texas. Reckon I'll save up enough working in the Arcade here to buy a passage over in a couple of months, but I shore do hate to miss the fighting."

"Well, Tom, I think I've given as much money to the Texas cause as any man in New Orleans. I guess I cannot let you down for lack of a few dollars." He writes a few sentences on two pieces of paper and hands them to you. "Those will get you a uniform and a gun," he says. "Use the gun shop on Water Street."

The uniform you are given is made of grey denim. It will wear well, the clothier tells you, because the material is tough and durable. The rush to supply the two companies going to Texas means that there is little time to alter the uniform. It is several sizes too large, but you figure that you can sew it up on the ship.

The gun shop on Water Street turns out to be one of the best in the city. Mr. Christy's note gets you immediate attention. The old gunsmith takes his time in finding you a rifle, a little shorter than most, but still almost as tall as you are. It is a fairly new flintlock.

"I hear that the Mexican army bought up a lot of old smooth bore muskets from the English navy," he tells you. "They ain't worth a tinker's dam over 50 yards. This here Kentucky flintlock you're taking is a lot more accurate and will kill a man at 200 yards."

Loaded down with the rifle, ammunition, and a bedroll and wearing the heavy grey uniform, you report to the docks at dawn on October 19. A steam ferry takes you out to the *Columbus* along with the rest of the company, which numbers just over sixty. There was a farewell party the night before, but it is too early for there to be much of a send-off this morning. Swiftly but gracefully, Captain Leidsdorf heads the *Columbus* downriver.

The three days aboard the little schooner seem more like a party than a potentially lethal journey to war. Spirits are high and there is a great deal of singing, raising toasts to Texas and liberty, and generally having a good time. Some of the men heave a chunk of bloody beef over the side, which draws sharks. Then everyone commences target practice, leaving a dark stain on the water as the sharks devour the carcasses of their kin as readily as anything else. You turn out to be a pretty good shot—which makes up for a lot of the teasing you endured the first day. The men

called you "the babe of the New Orleans Greys" and threatened to make you remain on the coast when the ship landed instead of going to join the Texas Army.

On that second day, though, a young man everyone called Connor took up for you. "See here, gentlemen, this backwoods babe from Arkansas can outshoot most of the men on this ship. Tom Benton," he said, turning to shake your hand, "you can march beside me in thick or thin."

Actually, Connor is not above 18 himself, and his confidence in your marksmanship is a lot greater than your own, but it is still comforting that someone is taking your side. You think how proud your brother Robert would be if he could see you now. Gradually the men come to accept you as a comrade, even if you are not quite their equal when it comes to quaffing beer or telling stories about the nightlife in New Orleans.

After a mere three days at sea, the watch calls out from one of the masts of the *Columbus*, "Land ho!" Within an hour the Texas coast is visible to all on board. Captain Leidsdorf's navigation is excellent — he only has to follow the coast line south for a few hours before you come to the twin port cities of Quintana and Velasco, located on either side of the mouth of the

Brazos River. It is October 22 when you walk down the gangway onto the McKinney and Williams wharf in the port of Velasco, on the southern shore of the Brazos. The Greys set up camp just outside the small town and spend the afternoon shooting prairie hens, partridges, and meadowlarks. The larks make for excellent target practice, being small and flighty, and the prairie hens make great eating that night, roasted on sticks over open fires. The men elect Robert C. Morris as captain of the New Orleans Greys.

The next morning a small steamboat, the *Laura,* takes the company swiftly upriver about twenty-five miles to the little city of Brazoria. The inhabitants of Brazoria have heard of your coming, and everyone for miles around turns out to welcome you to Texas. Mrs. Jane Long, the widow of the famous General Long who sought to free Texas from Mexico almost fifteen years before, has organized a feast for the Greys. As you walk through the town, a little cannon booms out a welcome and girls and young ladies wave their handkerchiefs, blow kisses, and throw an occasional flower at the men. It is a scene you will remember the rest of your life.

The Greys rise to the occasion and many stirring speeches are made by the men—

common, everyday men in New Orleans just three days ago—who now sound like conquering heroes about to engage in a battle to the death for the sake of liberty. You remember your grandfather telling about his experiences in the American Revolution—how even the most common farmboy seemed eloquent when it came to talking about freedom. You see the very same thing here, and it makes you proud. Captain Morris is treated like a bona fide hero, and as yet no one has fired a shot. Your friend Connor slips away from the doings with a girl, but pretty much everyone else stays close to the food and the wine.

The next day the company departs on foot for the town of Victoria, located some eighty miles west-southwest by the compass. Five days later your feet have learned the meaning of "march," but it is hard to complain: the country around is absolutely beautiful. Leaving the flat coastal plain, you enter some low rolling hills, most of which are crowned with mottes of oak and pecan trees. There is almost no need to hunt for game to eat—deer seem to be hiding in every little thicket you pass. Even if there were not enough meat, you could live on the abundant and delicious pecan nuts. In fact, a man could trail the Greys halfway across Texas, you think, just by following the pecan-shell path left behind.

Turn to page 89

PUBLIC MEETING

Public meeting tonight at eight o'clock in the Arcade. Liberty is at stake, the sovereignty of a people in whose veins flows the blood of the Anglo-Saxons. Texas, the prairie land, has arisen in order to oppose the tyrant, Santa Anna. The liberal citizens of the Union are being besought for aid. We have therefore instituted a general meeting of the inhabitants of our city and we hope to see our citizens in large numbers at the place.

"The Committee for Texas"

When you arrive at work on October 13, there is a large sign in front of the Arcade. It says "Public Meeting" in letters two feet high. Below it states that there will be a meeting tonight at the Arcade to talk about sending aid to the Texans fighting Mexico. Like almost everyone else, you think of Texas as being open land where anyone who can fight off the Indians ought to be able to stake a claim. From what the sign says, Mexico does not see it that way. You do not have to decide whether to go to the meeting or not; you will be serving drinks in the Arcade while the meeting goes on.

Even after working hard all day, when the heavy bells of the cathedral across the square toll out eight o'clock you are so excited that you do not feel tired at all. The Arcade, a huge place with a high ceiling supported with many columns, is filled with hundreds of men. The noise of their talking and shouting is tremendous, and a dense cloud of tobacco smoke is rising. At the sound of the bells, the speech making begins. Speaker after speaker is interrupted every two or three sentences by cheers, thunderous applause, and table thumping, even an occasional wild gunshot.

Texas, the speakers say, is rightfully governed by the 1824 Constitution of Mexico, which allowed colonists into Texas with very few restrictions—and no taxes to speak of. The Mexican government also promised that, when there were enough people settled in the region, it would become a separate state of Mexico. But Santa Anna, the new dictator of Mexico, will not even consider that. In fact, he put Stephen F. Austin in jail when Austin traveled to Mexico City to talk about it. The dictator then sent troops into Texas to collect his increasingly heavy import duties and to stop smuggling. Only ten days ago, on October 3, Santa Anna issued a decree that abolished all the state legislatures in the country, thus overthrowing the 1824 Constitution.

"All Mexico is in revolt against this tyranny," shouts a man from the platform. "But the Texans have the worst of it! Mexico wants their tax money, but won't send troops to fight off the Indians...."

A Texan in the crowd interrupts the speaker. Mexico *does* send troops to Texas, he says, but only to harass the colonists! In September, Santa Anna sent his brother-in-law, General Martín Perfecto de Cós, into Texas to settle a little dispute between the Anglo-American colonists and the Mexican authorities at a place called Anahuac. But Cós brought a whole army with him. "Now it looks very much like Santa Anna intends to occupy Texas with Mexican troops," the tall frontiersman says, "putting the whole region under martial law."

William Christy is a New Orleans businessman who has given so much aid to the Texas cause that he is being called the Lafayette of Texas after the French marquis who was so helpful to the American Revolution only fifty years before. Christy now tells the crowd at the Arcade that he has just received some news from Texas.

"At a place called Gonzales," he shouts, "the first shot of the Texas Revolution has been fired! One hundred and fifty Mexican soldiers were driven off by a small band of Texas volunteers when the Mexicans tried to take away a small cannon the people of Gonzales use for defense against the Indians. Can you believe it, gentlemen? What sort of government is so cruel as to abandon its citizens to the savage tribes of the prairies? But not only does Mexico abandon our brothers to this menace, it attempts to disarm them as well. How long shall this go on?"

The crowd breaks into cheers again. Christy goes on, telling about the money that has been raised and the men who are volunteering to fight for the Texas cause in cities like New York, Nashville, Mobile,

Cincinnati, and Louisville. Christy shouts out at last, "Shall we let these distant cities outstrip us, when we are so much nearer? When we understand the situation so much better?"

"No!" cries out a man near the front, throwing $50 in gold onto the platform. Others follow his example—before it is over, more than $10,000 in cash and pledges is raised in support of the Texas cause.

Finally another Texan steps onto the platform. Squire Adolphus Sterne, the *alcalde* of Nacogdoches, raises his voice above the crowd to say that Texas needs more than money. "Texas needs men," Sterne shouts. "Men willing to put their lives as well as their money on the line for liberty! I've just purchased fifty brand-new rifles. They belong to the first fifty men who will sign up to leave for Texas with me in the morning."

It so happens that you are near the stage when Squire Sterne makes his offer. A new rifle? A free trip to Texas? Adventure? You rush to the table to sign up along with more than a hundred others. At the table there are two men taking names. One is telling the men to be on board the riverboat *Washita* at dawn. That means heading up the Mississippi to the Red and over to Natchitoches. From there the company will have to travel on foot. The other man is saying that his group will sail in a few days across the Gulf of Mexico to the Texas port of Velasco. Going by sea seems like it would be quicker, but you are pretty sure that to get a free rifle you will have to join Sterne's group on the *Washita*.

If you decide to go by sea, turn to page 11

If you want to join Sterne on the riverboat, turn to page 43

Shortly after dawn, you are awakened by someone shaking your shoulder. "Look ma, he's half froze to death," a voice says. You try to get up, but your back feels as stiff as your gun barrel.

"Tom Benton, New Orleans Greys," you manage to mumble, but your teeth are chattering and your tongue seems too big for your mouth.

"What did he say, Dad?" asks a younger voice.

"Don't know, can't make it out. He's a pretty sick youngster, though. Got a heck of a fever. Reckon we'd better get him back to the cabin."

You remember all this like a dream—some of it is quite clear, and some of it is just a haze. For a long, long time, though, you seem to be floating, just waiting to wake up.

When you do wake up, you find that over a week has passed. Charlie MacReynolds, the farmer who found you beside the road, tells you that they expected you to die the first night.

"Yo're sure a tough 'un. Ma here kept you cooled down with spring water till the fever broke. Then you slept sound as a stone for nigh on three days. That's when we figured you weren't fixin' to die on us—that you must 'a been just plumb tuckered out. And here you are lookin' hungry as an old bear."

"Not quite," you say, "but I would like a little something, thank you."

Some food is brought by Mrs. MacReynolds, while Charlie chatters on. You find out that his oldest son has gone to join the Texas Army and is probably just now getting to San Antonio. They are very impressed that you are a member of the New Orleans Greys, but have trouble believing it until you manage to tell them the whole story from beginning to end.

"Young'un," Charlie says when you finish your story, "they's a whole lot of grown men ain't got yore kind of grit. I hope you stick around once the boys whip old Santy Anna. Texas is 'a gonna be needin' a lot of yore sort."

Tough you may be, but the fever has completely sapped your strength and it is Christmas before you feel well enough to think about rejoining the Greys. Mrs. MacReynolds and her red-haired daughter Trudi have tended you through the illness. You owe them a lot, but staying will not help them nearly so much as joining the army and freeing Texas. In the meantime, you learn that the Greys participated in the Siege of Bexar in early December, forcing General Cós to surrender. It was a difficult battle, lasting four full days and nights and involving house-to-house fighting. You wish you had been there and are anxious to be on your way.

There is one more thing you will owe this pioneer family. Mr. MacReynolds decides to give you a horse—he has just broken some wild mustangs to the saddle, and one of them is just about ready to ride. After Béxar fell, there seemed to be no need to hurry. General Cós was escorted across the Río Grande, having given his pledge never to cross it with troops again. Then you hear the awful news that all Texas has feared. General Antonio López de Santa Anna, the dictator of Mexico, is nearing the border with several thousand troops. You say good-bye to the MacReynolds, promise to say hello to their son if you can find him, and trot off down the road to Nacogdoches. You can see Trudi waving across this bit of cleared farmland and prairie for almost a mile. There's another girl you wonder whether you will ever see again. The prairie comes to an abrupt end as you enter the thick woods near Nacogdoches.

It is January 3 and the weather is extremely cold and windy. In Nacogdoches you pull up at the house of the *alcalde*, Adolphus Sterne, who is delighted to find

that you were not captured by Indians, as some of the Greys supposed when you did not show up. Some of them rode back the road a ways the morning after you disappeared, Mr. Sterne tells you, but, when you could not be found, the company rode on ahead. You are in a hurry to be off for San Antonio, but Mr. Sterne advises you to wait a day or so and to join the next group of volunteers that comes through. He fills you in on all the latest news, and you hear all about the incredible feast he spread for the Greys. There was even a whole roasted bear that they nicknamed "Mr. Petz."

You are impatient, but decide to wait in Nacogdoches as Mr. Sterne advises. It is certainly too cold to risk the journey alone when you are barely well, not to mention that the Nacogdoches–San Antonio Road runs far into Comanche territory. As it happens, the very next company of volunteers to ride into town is headed by none other than the famous Tennessee hunter, Indian fighter, and congressman Davy Crockett.

The whole town turns out once it is known who has arrived. The citizens fire off their cannon in welcome and yet another feast is prepared. That night the former congressman is in fine form. "I had rather be in my present situation than to be elected to a seat in Congress for life," he tells the crowd, which roars its approval. It is now common to administer an "oath of allegiance" to volunteers entering the state, and Judge John Forbes does the honors for Crockett. But when the judge is in the middle of reading the oath, Crockett stops him.

"Did I hear you say that I am promising to uphold any future government that you Texans might establish?" asks Crockett dramatically.

"Yes, indeed, you did," says Judge Forbes.

"Change that to 'any future *republican* government' and I'll sign it."

The judge writes in the change and Crockett signs it.

Crockett has with him an odd crew of volunteers—among them a gambler named Thimblerig, a gangly backwoodsman called Bee Hunter, an unlikely character named Micajah Autry who is a poet and violinist, and a couple of former pirates who were part of Jean Lafitte's old crew. And you are not the only volunteer in Nacogdoches who wants to ride to San Antonio with this living legend. John Purdy Reynolds, a doctor from Pennsylvania, and Daniel Cloud, Kentucky lawyer and idealist, are ready to join as well.

You cannot help but like Crockett. Full of anecdotes and backwoods humor, he is a big man who seems even bigger. At night he and Autry duel each other on the fiddle, passing it back and forth. "Come to My Bower" is his favorite song, and he likes to sing out loud while riding—an unusual trait for a hunter. You like him especially because he does not ask you about your age. "If you've got a rifle, a horse, and a will to fight for the right cause," he says, "I reckon I ain't the one to stop you riding with me."

You ride out two days later—quite proudly—as a member of Crockett's Tennessee Mounted Volunteers. The group takes its time, hunting along the way, talking and singing, always willing to sidle off the road to look at anything of interest in this new country. You have finally left the forests behind, and the wide prairies, with grass shoulder-high to your horse, are indeed fascinating, timeless almost. It reminds you a little of the floating feeling you had during your fever in Nacogdoches. Watching the wind-waves in the tall grass is hypnotic, and you begin to wonder whether you are falling ill again.

When you come to the little town of Bastrop, founded only four years before, you find several men recuperating from wounds they received in the skirmishes and battles around Béxar. Among them is a young man named Noah Smithwick, who greets Crockett's group from the small forge where he is working as a blacksmith. Smithwick fought at Gonzales and under Jim Bowie at the Battle of Concepción, but was taken with a fever shortly afterward. His forge draws every traveler coming through the small town, so you are able to find out a great deal about what has been happening in Béxar. On December 5 the Greys along with the rest of the Texas Army under Ben Milam and General Burleson finally attacked the Mexican forces in San Antonio. It was a hard-fought, house-to-house battle lasting four days that they are now calling the Siege of Béxar. Old Ben Milam was killed by a sniper, who shot him from one of the tall cypress trees growing along the Río San Antonio. General Cós himself holed up inside an old mission called San Antonio de Valero but which everyone refers to as the Alamo.

Turn to page 97

No one notices as you slip back into the stable and resaddle your horse. You know just how sick Connor is and that he might die from exposure if he really did pass out on the trail. Within a few minutes you are riding away from the *rancho,* back down the path you followed in. The night is abysmally dark, illuminated only for brief moments by lightning flashes. When you come to the place where the path to the *rancho* broke from the main track to Béxar, you realize that Connor must simply have followed the larger path. Maybe he is just lost, not lying unconscious and dying of exposure. You turn right toward Béxar and ride as fast as you can in the dark, occasionally calling out Connor's name.

You hear some sort of commotion up ahead. Dismounting, you tether your horse to a bush, dry out the pan on your rifle, and put in a fresh shake of gunpowder. The rifle itself is loaded, but in the rain the powder in the pan is almost always too wet to ignite unless it is fresh. Then you hear two, three, four shots sound dully in the heavy air. Forgetting caution, you run forward yelling, "Connor!"

Everything is confused as you suddenly come upon Connor, wrapped up in a blanket, with blood running down his chest. You turn just in time to see a Mexican soldier leveling his musket at you. Instinctively you fire without even raising the rifle to your shoulder. The soldier leaps backward, discharging his gun in the air. Before you can do anything else, two muskets belch fire from across the road. Your last thought as you fall next to the body of your friend is that it doesn't matter how inaccurate the muskets are when they are ten feet away.

For such a famous man, you think, Houston just does not stir you like Dr. Grant, whom Herman insists on calling "our beloved Scot." But Herman, surprisingly, will not join you. The Old General (Houston is 43), Herman decides, is looking at the larger picture; Dr. Grant, he says, is just interested in the pursuit of glory and silver. Thus Herman remains in Refugio while you ride away with Grant, Johnson, Morris, and 200 or so brave adventurers to meet Fannin at Copano. Fannin is to bring two new companies of volunteers from Georgia and Alabama—the Georgia Battalion and the Red Rovers—down to Copano from Velasco, where they landed.

But Fannin also decides that Houston is right, and the new volunteers are marched off to Refugio. From there Fannin intends to take them to Goliad along with anyone who will join him from the Refugio contingent.

In the meantime you arrive in the little settlement of Irish colonists, San Patricio de Hibernia. Most of the residents have fled, so you take up residence in one of the nicer adobe and log houses at the edge of town. You remain in San Patricio with Colonel Johnson and about fifty other men while Dr. Grant and Major

Morris take separate groups to round up some of the mustangs that run loose on the flat coastal plains.

Being the youngest member of the company, you quite often end up with the job of washing the cooking pots. After supper on February 27 you are doing just that at a nearby stream—scrubbing the pots Indian style with sand from the creek bed—when you hear shots from the town. You grab your rifle (you do not even wash dishes in this country without a gun handy) and run back up the hill, only to see a massacre going on. You cannot believe what you are seeing. It looks like your friends are being chased down by a lot of knights in armor. The Mexican soldiers at the Siege of Bexar looked nothing like this, but you remember hearing that the finest of the Mexican cavalry still wear armor and carry lances.

The moonlight glints off polished steel cuirasses and pointed helmets as the lancers ride down everyone in sight, spearing them and then tossing the bodies in the air. General Don José Urrea sweeps aside two Greys with his sword, leaving them to be finished off by the swarms of Mexican Indian infantry. It is too horrible to watch. Following the stream north, keeping to the densest part of the woods along its banks, you head for Goliad.

Turn to page 179

When you show up at the Mississippi River docks the next morning to board the *Washita,* it turns out that the little riverboat is not ready to leave—in fact, it will not leave for another couple of days. Mr. Sterne is there, though, and he is telling the volunteers where they can go to purchase some sturdy clothing. It seems that you are all going to wear grey uniforms of some sort. When you ask Mr. Sterne for the address of the clothier, he laughs.

"Aren't you a bit young to go fighting Mexicans, son?" he asks.

"No, sir!" you reply. "I come all the way down the Ouachita, the Red, and the Mississippi by myself in a dugout canoe," you tell him, proud of the feat, you have to admit.

"You came all that way by yourself just to join the fight for Texas?" Mr. Sterne asks.

"I did indeed," you lie, thinking that the truth—that your father had every intention of pretending you were a mule for the next ten years—would not sound either very brave or very soldierish. "I know I'm a little small for my age, but I aim to make it all the way to San Antone and marry me a pretty señorita there like they say Jim Bowie did."

You are not at all sure how such a lie came out of your mouth, but you pinch

yourself to keep a straight face as Mr.
Sterne looks you over.

"Can you shoot?" he asks.

"I can," you say, bold as brass, "but not
without a rifle."

After what seems like an awfully long
time, Mr. Sterne says, "Well, I'm not at all
sure you're old enough to be thinking
about pretty señoritas, but you seem determined enough, and that counts for a lot."

"I'm as old as my grandfather was when
he fought 'side Gen'l Washington," you tell
him. That, at least, is the truth, and it gives
you a warm feeling inside when you think
about it. Freeing Texas from a Mexican dictator is not very different at all from freeing the American colonies from King
George.

"Am I in?" you ask.

"You're in."

He checks you off his list and hands you
the clothier's address and a brand new flintlock rifle that is almost as tall as you are.

Your employer at Bank's Arcade is sur-
prised that Mr. Sterne has agreed to take
you, but he agrees to pay for your uniform
and sends you off, wishing you good luck.
After getting the grey uniform, which is far
too big, you spend the rest of your money
on gunpowder, a bullet mold, shot lead, and
other things you will need. While waiting

for the *Washita* to be made ready, you get some leather and sew up a case for your rifle and a sheath for your brother Robert's big dirk knife.

The *Washita*'s steam engine is already billowing black smoke over the dock when you arrive. It is early in the morning, October 17, 1835. Everyone all over New Orleans seems caught up in the campaign to support the cause of Texas freedom. Many are already going beyond the idea of making Santa Anna reestablish the Constitution of 1824—they are talking about forming a new country, the Republic of Texas. These are exciting times indeed. One of the five daily newspapers in New Orleans has published a list of the men leaving on the *Washita* this morning. You read the list carefully and, yes, there it is: Thomas Benton. You are delighted to see your name in print. The last thing you do before boarding is to tear out the list and put it in an envelope addressed to your brother Robert back in Arkansas.

The dock is lined with well-wishing ladies and gentlemen as well as cheering dock hands when the *Washita* heads upriver. The cheering is soon lost, though, in the puffing of the engine and the river sounds. Around you are the volunteers who will travel with you all the way to Texas. They

hail from a dozen different states, and several have only recently arrived in America from Europe. But one and all, they are dedicated to the cause of freedom and liberty. Like you, many of those from the states talk proudly of their grandfathers who were veterans of the American Revolution, and several have fathers who fought in the War of 1812.

All the way up the Mississippi to the juncture with the Red River, then on up the Red past where the Ouachita runs into it, you watch for the landmarks you saw in your canoe. It already seems like a long, long time ago that you were paddling south on these waters.

After leaving the wide expanse of the Mississippi, the Red River seems narrow and cramped, with the junglelike forest hanging over the thick, turbid, reddish waters. You and your companions spend the long days practicing with the new rifles by shooting at the hundreds of alligators that line the banks. Very soon you have the loading routine down: pour the powder (two shakes out of the powder horn into the muzzle of the rifle) followed by a bit of wadding and the bullet, really a ball. The load is tamped down with the ramrod, then the pan is primed with a bit more gunpowder. When you pull the trigger, the piece of flint in the hammer hits a striker over the pan, making a spark that ignites the powder in the pan, which ignites the load in the barrel and fires the gun.

Besides yourself, the youngest member of the company is a German boy of about 18 named Herman Ehrenberg. He is also a runaway, he tells you, but from much further away. He was a student at the University of Jena in Germany, but decided he would rather see the world for himself rather than just reading about it.

It seems to you that Herman is just about the smartest fellow you ever met. You are convinced that there is no subject about which Herman couldn't talk your ear off — except shooting. Like you, he has the loading and firing down, but neither of you has come closer than a couple of feet away from one of the alligators on the bank.

Some of the older men, however, are experienced Indian fighters and can shoot squirrels out of the trees fifty yards away. Together you and Herman listen as they correct your mistakes. Peter Mattern and Henry Curtman, two other young Germans just a little older than Herman, enjoy themselves greatly during these practice sessions.

"You better hope the Mexicans are easier to hit than alligators," laughs Henry,

" 'cause they aren't going to give you as many second chances as them 'gators."

It is true. You could blast away all day and, unless you actually hit one, the big old monsters would hardly turn their heads at you. By the time the *Washita* ties up at the little village of Alexandria on the Red River, you have gotten much better—at the expense of a very sore shoulder.

At Alexandria the people have been alerted to the coming of the First Company of the New Orleans Greys, as the group is now called. Mr. Sterne came upriver as few days before the *Washita* departed, so all the folk of Alexandria are out on the docks and there is quite a feast. It is just a little river village, quite like the ones near your home in Arkansas, and the hour or so the Greys spend there is probably the most exciting thing the village ever witnessed.

Turn to page 69

Tired as you are, you know that spending the night in the open when you are already wet and cold will result in a fever or worse. Stumbling along for another couple of miles, you come to the end of the small prairie and enter the forest once again. It is a bit warmer in the woods—at least the wind cannot get to you here.

Another hour brings you to the outskirts of Nacogdoches. The first house you come to is surrounded by horses and light shines from every window. It is an unusually large house for a frontier dwelling, and you suspect that it must belong to Mr. Sterne, the town's *alcalde* or mayor.

Herman greets you at the door. "Well, wayfaring stranger! We were getting worried that you'd run into some trouble."

"No. I just rested for a spell. Almost went to sleep with the cold and all."

"I am delighted that you woke up, then," Herman says as he helps you find a place at the crowded table. "We would have had to thaw you out over a fire if you'd stayed out on that prairie all night."

A hot cup of coffee warms you up and clears your head. Herman and his fellow German countrymen among the Greys are delighted when Mr. Sterne produces some excellent German Rhine wine. While you eat, an interesting debate develops when Henry Curtman proposes a toast, which ends, "as a citizen of the new state I pledge you my last drop of human blood . . ."

Sterne at once cries out, "Halt, my countryman. Quiet! Do you wish to stir up the whole of Mexico against us?" There is still a chance of reinstating the Constitution of 1824, he tells the group, though open rebellion is not out of the question if Santa Anna refuses to compromise. This plunges the whole company into a hot debate. Mr. Sterne argues that the Texas Army is not yet strong enough to take on the several armies of Mexico, a conflict that will inevitably arise if talk of U.S. statehood or an independent republic continues.

Most of the Greys side with Henry, however, saying that they did not come all the way to Texas just to help Mexico settle internal affairs. Many of the Greys talk openly of "driving every brown-skinned Meskin in Texas into the Río Grande." This does not strike you as very sensible, as you have often heard how friendly the Tejanos, Texans of Mexican or Spanish ancestry, have been to the colonists from the United States and Europe. There are probably a lot of Tejanos in the Texas Army, you think. It is an argument, however, that no one will listen to—especially coming from a 14-year-old Arkansas farmboy. Later, far past midnight, Sterne takes the company on a short tour of Nacogdoches. He stops at the local tavern, pointing out the "Mexicans" who provide the entertainment, run the gambling room, and work behind the bar. He seems to think that this proves something bad about all Mexicans. It seems odd to you that he does not mention that the card sharks working the tables and most of the drunken crowd are Anglo-Americans.

The next day, the women of the town are busy the better part of the day preparing a great "feast of liberty."

"I'm beginning to think I ain't going to mind these marches at all," you say to Herman, "if'n they all end in feasts like this one here!"

It is true—Mr. Sterne and the citizens of Nacogdoches have spread a huge feast on a line of tables nearly 150 feet long, which runs down the town's main street. On either side bonfires burn—the norther that blew through has left a decided chill in the air. The tables are loaded with a whole roasted bear, turkey, and fried raccoon, and tall glasses of Rhine wine. Herman and his fellow countrymen are delighted. The dinner is something of a Bowie knife free-for-all, since there are few forks on hand. But the plates are of white china and the glasses are crystal.

Again there are speeches and toasts and arguments over what Texas will become, but mostly there is eating. The next morning, there are a lot of headaches from the wine. Herman, Henry, and Peter insisted that, in honor of their homeland, you try the Rhine wine. Thus, you also, awaken with a throbbing head.

From Nacogdoches on, the Greys are a cavalry troop, owing to the acquisition of horses—mostly half-wild mustangs—from the citizenry. Except for having to chase down loose horses every so often, the Greys make steady progress, crossing the Angelina and Trinity rivers and moving through the last of the dense forests and out onto the rolling hills and open stretches of prairie. The changing colors of the trees are beautiful, and there are pecan nuts in abundance. It seems that every man of the company has a bag of these delicious nuts, which are shelled and eaten while riding.

Herman says that the gently rolling hills, crowned by mottes of oak and pecan, remind him of the royal parklands of Europe. Every little stream is lined with trees, forming what the Tejanos call *galerias*. You have to admit that the steep hills of Arkansas seem cramped compared with these wide open spaces. At Washington-on-the-Brazos you find a hive of activity, as if you can see the town visibly getting larger from day to day. A little further, you come to an extensive pine forest. It is a relief to be in the woods again, because the plains in this area are still the preserve of the Comanche Indians, some of the fiercest warriors on earth. As beautiful as the country is, however, you are having difficulty appreciating it. The headache you awoke with in Nacogdoches is still with you, proving that it is more than just a first hangover. Pretty soon you are sneezing and enduring chills that seem to come and go. Evidently you did catch a cold that night before you reached Nacogdoches.

Late one night the company emerges from the forest atop a hill overlooking the small town of Bastrop, founded only a few years before in 1832 by Miguel Arciniega. Before that, Señor Arciniega had been the *alcalde* of Béxar. His gallantry, hospitality, and patriotism toward Texas rather than Mexico go a long way toward settling the anti-Tejano feelings the men expressed back in Nacogdoches.

Bastrop welcomes the Greys with bonfires and fresh news. Two weeks before, on October 28, a group of 92 Texas volunteers under Jim Bowie and James Fannin defeated 300 of General Cós's troops at a mission called Concepción just a couple of miles south of San Antonio. The Texans lost one man, while the Mexican army suffered over 60 killed and 40 wounded. The Mexican troops used a cannon and made several cavalry charges against the Texans, who were positioned in the cover of the brush and trees along a bend of the Río San Antonio. The Mexican infantrymen were using old British smooth-bore muskets that are notoriously inaccurate. The Kentucky flintlocks of the Texans cut them down with deadly accuracy from almost 100 yards. Even now the Texas Army had General Cós's whole force bottled up inside San Antonio de Béxar.

Staying in Bastrop are a couple of men who only recently came from Béxar with more recent news: Stephen F. Austin, the leader of the Texas Army, has been elected by the Consultation at San Felipe de Austin to represent the Texan cause in the United States. Austin has already left

San Antonio, and now General Edward Burleson is in charge of the siege. Apparently they are waiting for the arrival of some cannon before making an assault upon Cós.

The Greys are excited, ready to make the 100-mile trek from Bastrop to San Antonio across the prairies ruled only by the Comanches. Everyone wants to get to Béxar before the cannon in order to join the fight. Herman, however, presses you to remain in Bastrop until you feel better. A midwinter cold, with few doctors and less medicine to be had, can get very nasty if it turns into pneumonia. A man named Noah Smithwick is also down with a fever in Bastrop. Smithwick, a blacksmith, scout, and sometime smuggler in his mid-20s, fought at Gonzalez and at Concepción and is full of stories, sick as he is. He has every intention of heading south again as soon as he can sit a horse. Noah also urges you to stay and recuperate.

"Forget all that glare and glitter business you've read about war in the storybooks," he tells you. "War is a dirty job and there's no room for sick folk like us. You just stick it out with old Noah here and we'll get back into the fight in no time, you'll see."

You are pretty sick, but you are also sure you can make it to San Antonio. You would hate to miss out on the battle that is sure to occur there in a few days.

If you decide to stay in Bastrop with Noah, turn to page 63

If you decide to go on to Béxar with the Greys, turn to page 155

The town is strangely empty. Following the course of the river, holding your rifle and powder horn above the water, you wade down the winding San Antonio. The pain in your leg is excruciating, but worse is the doubt you feel about leaving the Alamo. You shouldn't have let yourself be convinced that just because you are so young you should not stick it out. You've been in battles, you've killed Mexican soldiers, you have a right to fight beside men like Crockett and Bowie. Just as

you are about to turn around and go back to the Alamo, you see a big black swirling shape in the water. Water moccasin. You swing the rifle butt at it, sending the snake up onto the bank. *"Ai! Gringo. Muerte!"* a gruff voice snarls from the trees. There is a blinding flash, and you know no more.

The argument is put to rest when Captain Breeze orders you to stay in Bastrop. You are afraid that he is only ordering you to stay to keep you out of the battle. He has said several times that he thinks both you and Herman are too young to be soldiers.

This time, however, he makes it clear that he is giving you a military order—one not to be disobeyed. "Private Benton, I fully expect you to rejoin the Greys within the month. Driving General Cós out of San Antonio won't be the end of this war in Texas. Sooner or later we will have to face old Santa Anna himself, and I expect we will be needing your rifle then."

Throughout December you do your best to get over the fever, which in fact does turn worse for a while. After Christmas, however, you are able to help Noah at a small blacksmith shop where he is working. Pumping the bellows is good exercise for you, and the shop is actually a lot warmer than the house where you and he have been staying. The forge draws every traveler coming through the small town, so you are able to keep up on the news from Béxar. On December 5 the Greys along with the rest of the Texas Army under Ben Milam and General Burleson gave up on ever getting the large cannon they had been waiting for and attacked the Mexican forces in San Antonio. It was a hard-fought, house-to-house battle. Old Ben Milam was killed by a sniper, who shot him from one of the tall cypress trees that grow along the river running through Béxar.

General Cós himself holed up inside an old mission called San Antonio de Valero, which everyone refers to as the Alamo. Even though he still had a superior force in numbers, Cós surrendered when he found himself trapped in the Alamo. You wonder how Herman and Peter and Henry and the rest of the Greys fared in the battle. General Burleson received a promise from General Cós, according to the formal rules of warfare, that Cós would retire beyond the Río Grande, never to take up arms against Texas again. Noah just spat when he heard about the terms of the surrender. "Them rules of warfare aren't going to matter a whit to Santa Anna when he gets here. We'll see Cós in Texas again, you mark my words."

Others folks seemed to think the war was over. Many of the Texas volunteers in San Antonio left the army to go see about their farms and to spend Christmas with their families—even General Burleson himself—and some of the wounded settled for a while in Bastrop until the situation became clear as to where they would be needed. The spoils of the Siege of Béxar were not insignificant either—some of the Texans passing through were sitting on fancy silver-mounted Mexican saddles and were wearing huge-roweled silver spurs.

The most exciting news is that almost 200 men marched out of San Antonio on December 30 with Dr. James Grant, intent on carrying the war into Mexico by attacking Matamoros. Most of the Greys went on this expedition, including the Second Company of Greys from New Orleans, who signed up that same night at Bank's Arcade but traveled to Texas by ship across the Gulf.

Noah has nothing but scorn for Dr. Grant, claiming that the shrewd Scot led the expedition into Mexico solely to regain possession of some estates that were confiscated by the government. All this left San Antonio de Béxar and the Alamo under the command of Colonel James C. Neill, who had scarcely 100 men and very few arms or supplies. Grant not only drew off most of the men but commandeered every weapon worth taking in the city.

But not everyone is leaving San Antonio. In mid-January you are delighted to see the most famous frontiersman alive riding into Bastrop at the head of a little group of volunteers. Davy Crockett—Indian fighter, bear hunter, congressman, and living legend—is standing at the door of your forge, asking if you can shoe his horse.

Crockett, who followed basically the same road into Texas that you did through San Augustine and Nacogdoches, has with him an odd crew of volunteers. There is a gambler named Thimblerig, a gangly backwoodsman called Bee Hunter, a couple of old ex-pirates who served with Jean Lafitte in New Orleans twenty years before, and an unlikely character named Micajah Autry who is a poet and plays the violin. Daniel Cloud, a lawyer from Kentucky, joined up with Crockett in Nacogdoches, as did a doctor, John Purdy Reynolds, originally from Pennsylvania.

You are tired of sitting around—or rather you are tired of standing around pumping the forge bellows—so you ask Crockett to take you along with him. He does not even question your age. "If you've got a rifle, a horse, and a will to fight for the right cause," he says, "I reckon I ain't the one to stop you ridin' with me."

Noah, on the other hand, is still up and down with the fever. "You go on," he tells you, "I think your time is at hand. Shore do wish I was up to joining you though."

You say good-bye to Noah and Bastrop, saddle up, and ride out the following day with Colonel Davy Crockett, proud as you can be.

Turn to page 75

A few days more on the Red River brings the *Washita* to the bustling little town of Natchitoches. Again the Greys are met by most of the town's population at the dock. By this time the Greys have elected Thomas Breeze as the company's captain, and he orders the company to march off the riverboat in double columns. It is your first time as a real soldier, you think, though marching is the easiest part of it. The Greys set up camp in the forest just outside of town, to which the citizens of Natchitoches bring gifts of food and other supplies all that evening and the next morning.

"I don't know how we're ever going to carry all this stuff," you say to Herman.

"So try and eat more of it and you won't have to carry it," he replies, enjoying a roasted chunk of venison as he talks.

About two in the afternoon Captain Breeze rides up, shouting orders to break camp as soon as possible. Word has just arrived, he says, that the Texas volunteer army has decided to move against General Cós in San Antonio de Béxar. Everyone hurries—no one wants to get there after the battle. Since you still have to cross some 300 miles of Texas forests and prairies, there is no time to lose. After ten hours on the march, you are beginning to

have second thoughts about marching being the easiest part of soldiering. By midnight you are exhausted. Captain Breeze says you are quite near the Sabine River —and across the Sabine lies Texas.

You reach Gaines's Ferry on the Sabine the next morning. Across the river there is quite a crowd. Herman, Peter, and Henry are enthusiastic as you cross over on the hand-pulled ferry barge. "Look at the girls," says Henry. "They're all wearing their best dresses to welcome us to Texas." Despite your talk of pretty señoritas, you have a hard time not laughing at Herman and his friends combing their hair and twisting their moustaches. Unlike the Red, the Sabine is a beautifully clear and calm river, and the sun makes it mirror-bright. Then, staring beyond the glare, you see her. The prettiest girl you ever dreamed of is standing on the shore holding a big blue flag. When the ferry ties up, she welcomes Captain Breeze in the name of all Texans and presents him with the flag. It is made of rich blue silk with gold fringe, about four feet by six feet, with an eagle in the middle that carries in its beak a streamer reading "God and Liberty." Above and below the eagle is written, "First Company of Texas Volunteers from New Orleans."

It is all very emotional, and some of the men even bend down to kiss the ground of this place you have come to fight for, maybe die for. After a short speech thanking the ladies for their hard work in making the flag, Captain Breeze orders the company into a brisk march. With the flag flying at the front of the column, and the cheering behind, you feel very proud to be with these men. Even if you have to die in the attempt, you think, it will be worth it to keep these people free. As the company marches away from the Sabine, you wonder what the girl's name was, and if you will ever see her again.

The road, just a few feet wider than a single wagon, is clear of brush and fairly straight. Cut directly through the dense forests of Louisiana and East Texas by the Spanish over a hundred years ago, it was called El Camino Real, the King's Road. Running from Natchitoches on the Red River to Nacogdoches and down to San Antonio de Béxar, it is now called the San Antonio–Nacogdoches Road and is the main route for settlers entering Texas. The company makes excellent time—two day's march brings you to the little town of San Augustine.

Upon approaching the little town, you hear the sound of a military drum beat.

The Greys' drummer beats out a lively response. Pretty soon you see the members of the San Augustine militia marching out to meet you. They join your column and together you march into the market square in San Augustine. Three small cannon boom out a welcome, and suddenly you are surrounded by the succulent aroma of hot food. A whole beef is roasting over a pit, and there are tables with white tablecloths loaded down with an assortment of hearty frontier fare.

That evening a norther howls in that drops the temperature and makes you glad that you are being put up in the citizens' cabins rather than camping out in the cold. You, Henry, and Peter are staying with an old man who spends the evening prodding the fire and telling you stores about fighting the British with General Jackson at New Orleans in the War of 1812. You find it very interesting, but roll up in a bearskin rug and fall asleep while the stories go on and on.

Two days later, late in the evening, you find yourself at the tail end of the column, getting further and further behind. Captain Breeze gave the company permission to break ranks, allowing everyone to walk at his own speed, so the company is now stretched out over several miles. Just fol-

74

low the road, they said, but you have come to a prairie – the first you have ever seen – and the road is not very clear in the dim light. It is bitterly cold and the wind is cutting right through the "sturdy frontier-proof clothing" that seemed so heavy back in New Orleans. What *is* heavy is your rifle. Your shoulder feels like it has an inch-deep groove where you have carried it all day. Finally, frozen to the bone and thoroughly miserable, you decide that, no matter how late it is, you will sit down and take a rest. After a while you notice that your toes are getting numb. Unrolling the buffalo hide given you by the old man in San Augustine, you wrap up and try to get warm. You know Nacogdoches can't be too many miles ahead, but the thought of going any further that night makes you ache all over.

If you decide to camp alone on the prairie for the night, turn to page 27

If you decide to get up and walk on to Nacogdoches now, turn to page 51

Crockett's Tennessee Mounted Volunteers, hailing from half a dozen places besides Crockett's home state, fairly fly south to San Antonio de Béxar. Knowing just how badly you are needed there drives the fever right out of you, replacing it with furious energy.

Despite the hurry of this final dash to San Antonio, once there the "coonskin congressman" stops off at the cantina in the town plaza before riding out to the Alamo itself, where what is left of the Texas Army is busy turning the old mission into a fort. Within minutes of your arrival, townspeople and soldiers begin to show up at the cantina to get a look at the most famous frontiersman alive. Pretty soon even the garrison commanders, Colonel Neill, Jim Bowie, and William Barret Travis, arrive. Someone calls for a speech and Crockett willingly obliges, standing on some crates in the plaza.

It is at once a hilarious and very stirring speech. Crockett mixes backwoods humor and patriotic sentiments into the kind of sentences that roll around your head for weeks. But he concludes soberly, saying, "All the honor that I desire is that of defending as a high private, in common with my fellow citizens, the liberties of our common country."

Go on to the next page

For a few days after Crockett's arrival there is a round-the-clock fandango. Crockett just seems to inspire such things. Since you have eaten periodic feasts all along the way to Béxar yourself, this fandango seems almost a natural conclusion. Pretty señoritas dance, beating out exotic rhythms with their heels, guitars ring out, Crockett tells his tall tales, and the throat-searing *ron blanco* pours endlessly. Then, at one in the morning, February 12, a messenger rides up, his horse heavily lathered and covered with mud. He insists on seeing Colonel Erasmo Seguín, but the old and highly respected Tejano is not likely to be found in the plaza cantina in the middle of the night. The message is delivered to Colonel Travis, who, as it happens, *is* in the plaza cantina in the middle of the night.

The message is from Captain Placido Benavides, who reports that he has certain knowledge that Santa Anna is marching with some 13,000 men—and that he is headed directly for San Antonio de Béxar. Travis, Bowie, and Crockett discuss the message, but decide that there is no need to call a halt to the party. The next morning, Colonel Neill, who was not consulted about the Benavides message, announces that he has been called away to attend to an illness in his family. He passes command of the garrison to young Buck Travis—Colonel William Travis to anyone who is not also a colonel, even though the uniform which Travis ordered has never arrived. Hardly anyone notices that Neill has left.

On the other hand, Jim Bowie and his men are fired up to a drunken pitch over who is actually in command. Bowie makes it clear that he thinks Travis, who has only been there a week and is 26 years old, is unfit for such an important post. Everything is confused until, quite suddenly, on the fourteenth, Travis and Bowie agree to a simple split: Travis will command the army regulars, Bowie the volunteers, and all the big decisions will be mutually agreed upon.

Colonel Jim Bowie, one of the commanders at the Battle of Concepción and a fierce fighter during the Siege of Béxar, is almost as famous a character as Davy Crockett. Known for his wickedly effective use of the large knife that bears his name, he does not now cut the figure you expected. His men are all extremely loyal to him, yet he is very moody, a gaunt

loner with a haunted look. Three years earlier his wife and children died during a cholera epidemic, and Bowie's friends claim he has never been the same since. Now Bowie is apparently suffering from some sort of illness, which he compounds by indulging his considerable capacity for whiskey.

The garrison consists of some 140 men now, only a few of them Greys. Word comes that the expedition against Matamoros was met with considerable force, and that a lot of Texans were killed. You wonder about Herman and the rest of the New Orleans Greys who went with Dr. Grant, but there is so much to do in the Alamo that you cannot spend much time worrying about them. For some reason, though, they left behind the big blue silk flag that the beautiful girl gave to Captain Breeze at the Sabine River. The flag is hanging inside the mission church. Over the walls flies the Mexican tricolor flag, with "1824" printed in the middle — something of a taunt to the dictator whose overthrow of the 1824 Constitution of Mexico brought on the rebellion he is even now marching north to quell.

Meanwhile, work goes on. The mission, already over eighty-five years old, consists of a large rectangular plaza, which encloses a little more than one acre. It is surrounded by an assortment of walls and buildings. Along the south side of the plaza run the "low barracks," through which the Alamo's main gate opens. To the west and north there is a strong, twelve-foot-high stone wall against which several adobe huts have been built. A portion of the eastern side of the plaza consists of a two-story building called the "long barracks." The other part of the eastern side is open ground facing the mission church, which is set back from the plaza some twenty to thirty yards. Between the church and the low barracks there is only a half-finished wooden palisade backed by earthworks.

The most imposing structure is the church itself, but even that is a pretty sorry sight. Only a few timbers remain of the chapel roof, though there are a couple of rooms still intact. General Cós tried to fortify the place during his stay, mainly by building an earthen ramp that ran up to a platform on the eastern end where cannon could be placed. As soon as the Texans determined to hold the Alamo rather than blow it up as General Houston ordered Bowie to do, Colonel Neill and Bowie began building scaffolding along the walls. The tops of the walls, however, are perfectly flat, with no embrasures to shoot from and nothing to hide behind. Shooting over the wall will mean presenting a perfect target to the attacking Mexicans.

Your first and almost continuous job in the Alamo is helping to saw timbers for the scaffolding. The other end of the two-handled crosscut saw is often handled by John McGregor, who whistles the airs and jigs of his native Scotland in time with the saw. Green Jameson, the Alamo engineer, is constantly calling for more wood—there are more platforms to be raised, and scaffolding is still incomplete. The southwest corner emplacement for the Alamo's heaviest cannon, an eighteen-pounder, is only half finished. When Jameson is not demanding more wood, he is calling for more dirt. As thick as the walls are, almost all need earthen bracing if they are to withstand a substantial cannonade.

More messages come in over the next few days warning of Santa Anna's approach. Blas Herrera, a cousin of Captain Juan Seguín and a member of the gallant San Antonian's company of Tejanos, reports on February 20 that he himself saw Santa Anna's army crossing the Río Grande six or seven days before. Benavides's earlier report that Santa Anna has

13,000 men turns out to be an exaggeration, and it is certain that the Mexican forces have dwindled considerably on the long march north. The most reliable reports now estimate the Mexican force at around 5,000. Some men predict the arrival of the Mexicans any day, but most are convinced that such a large army will move pretty slowly. It was only a week ago that a blizzard swept out of the north, blanketing the plains in snow, and that was quickly followed by torrential rains. Surely, everyone says, all the rivers are flooded.

But no matter what anyone believes about when Santa Anna will arrive, the business of fortifying the Alamo and preparing for his arrival goes on. Captain Almeron Dickinson, a blacksmith from Gonzales, drills a company of men daily on the eighteen cannon in the fort, which range in size from those hurling a small four-pound shot to the big eighteen-pounder. Hiram Williamson drills the general soldiers on everything from rapid loading to how to get on and off the scaffolding without knocking each other off. Supplies begin to appear—42 head of cattle, 100 bushels of corn, gunpowder and lead. Sam Blair, a Tennessean, has begun collecting every piece of scrap metal

in Béxar—including every horseshoe not attached to a horse—which he chops into pieces to use as cannon shot, cannonballs being in short supply.

On February 16 Travis sends the best horse and horseman in the Alamo, Major James Bonham, with a message to Colonel Fannin at Goliad. It is rumored that Fannin has over 400 men—some of them remnants of the Matamoros expedition and some recruits and volunteers newly arrived from all over the United States. They are fortifying the Presidio at La Bahía, which Fannin has renamed Fort Defiance. You hope Bonham is persuasive—things are beginning to get grim in Béxar. If the reports are right, Santa Anna is moving north more quickly than anyone imagined.

Whether or not Bonham succeeds in bringing Fannin's force to Béxar, you realize that the arrival of Santa Anna cannot be far off when, on February 21, you see local citizens loading their belongings and children into wooden-wheeled ox carts that can be heard squeaking all over town. Later that evening couriers ride in with the latest reports: Santa Anna himself is on the banks of the Medina River, less than twenty-five miles from the Alamo.

On February 23 you find yourself helping search the houses of the departed citizens for arms and food. That morning more and more citizens take to the roads, their ox carts piled high. "Time to start spring planting," they answer when asked where they are going. A little after noon the bell in the tower of the San Fernando cathedral, on Main Plaza, begins ringing wildly. It is the signal that the enemy is in sight; but when several men reach the top of the tower, there is nothing to be seen. The sentry swears that he saw the polished armor of Santa Anna's cavalry shining in the sun. Travis sends out two men, John Sutherland and John Smith, to confirm the sighting. Everyone is on edge, and you catch yourself holding your breath for long stretches at a time. Hardly anyone is actually inside the Alamo, but when Sutherland and Smith come riding hell for leather into Main Plaza, there is a sudden rush for the old mission.

"Poor fellows," an old woman says as you pass by. "You will all be killed."

Captain Dickinson gallops past you and comes to a quick stop in front of the Musquiz home where his wife is staying. "Quick, Sue," he calls out. "Give me the baby! Jump on behind and ask me no questions."

Jim Bowie's two sisters-in-law, Juana and Gertrudis Veramendi, leave their home headed for the safety of the Alamo and Bowie's personal protection. Several other citizens enter the mission. There are a pretty señorita, Trinidad Saucedo, an old market woman, and others.

Turn to page 101

Once Captain Morris takes charge of the company, things begin to get more orderly. Sentries are stationed each night to guard the camp and the few pack horses. Roving patrols of Mexican soldiers are supposed to be in the area, but more likely—and more dangerous—are Indian raiding parties. You are up at first light every morning and marching within the hour. The eighty miles to the town of Guadalupe Victoria stretches to a hundred when the twists in the road—often little more than a path—are taken into account, not to mention having to cross several streams and a couple of good-sized rivers. Still, you do reach Victoria on November 1.

Once again, you are amazed at the kind of party such a small town can muster. This time the festivities are presided over by Mrs. Margaret C. Linn and Miss Susan Linn, two Irish ladies who add a certain gaiety lacking at Mrs. Long's rather formal reception. There is plenty to eat and drink, with music and dancing. Connor takes up with one of the señoritas and introduces you to another. About your age, with raven hair and dark brown eyes, she is about the prettiest creature you have ever seen. The women make a considerable fuss over both of you, especially when

Captain Morris's second-in-command, Lieutenant William Cooke, gives a rousing speech in which he promises that every last drop of the Greys' blood will be spent, if necessary, in the defense of Texas.

After little sleep that night, but greatly fortified by the food and good feelings, the Greys resume their march late the next morning. The good citizens of Victoria give a parting gift in the form of several wild mustangs. But the gift proves dangerous.

"Considering how many bruised bottoms and busted heads these mustangs have given the company," Connor says to you a couple of days later, nursing a bruised shoulder himself, "seems to me not all them Mexican folk back in Victoria are on our side."

It is true that most of the citizens of Victoria originally came from Mexico, some even from Spain, but they call themselves Tejanos and are clearly as upset with the overtaxation and military rule as the American and European immigrants to the region. It is also true that the mustangs are more than a little difficult to ride, but you point out to Connor that every good saddle horse in the town is in use—and probably in the service of the

Texas Army. Why else are there so many women and so few men in these towns? "Besides," you tell him, "I thought you were in love with the señoritas of Guadalupe Victoria." Connor disagrees on a number of points, and a lively argument keeps the two of you occupied throughout the rest of that day's march.

The company is now getting close to the mission/fort called Presidio la Bahía near Goliad. You find that the name "Goliad" is really the Texas pronunciation of *Goliat,* which is Spanish for "Goliath." The name came from the size and strength of the presidio. Before arriving in Victoria, the plan had been to join the Texas Army near Goliad and help take the fort from the Mexicans. But at Victoria you learned that La Bahía fell almost a month before on October 9, to a Captain Collinsworth and a band of volunteers. The Texans had attacked in the middle of the night, sneaking past a sleepy sentry and taking it by surprise. One Mexican was killed, one Texan wounded. The Mexican garrison at La Bahía was small, but the bounty the fort yielded was rich—two cannon, hundreds of muskets, powder, food, and horses. Captain Collinsworth then returned to San Antonio with most of his men, leaving the place under Captain Dimmitt.

The captain's scouts have reported that
the Greys are approaching, and he has
rounded up enough horses for the whole
company. They are of much better qual-
ity than the mustangs from Victoria,
though equally wild. It seems that if you
are going to ride horseback in Texas, you
had better get used to breaking horses.

Captain Dimmitt and his men also tell
the company about the recent events in
San Antonio. Only a few days before, on
October 28, Jim Bowie's troop of *leoncitos*—the little lions—and James Fannin's Brazos Guards fought a battle with
some of General Cós's troops at a mission
just south of San Antonio de Béxar called
Concepción.

"They're warming up for the big one,"
Dimmitt says. "You all better get on up to
Béxar if you want to be part of it."

The Battle of Concepción was a small
affair really, with the forces coming
together almost by accident in an early
morning fog, but the Mexican losses,
some 60 killed and 40 wounded out of a
force of 300 compared to the Texans' loss
of a single man, is heartening news. You
remember what the old gunsmith in New
Orleans told you about the effectiveness
of the Mexican muskets. Dimmitt agrees,
saying that "one sharp-eyed Texan with a

Kentucky rifle is worth five or more Mexicans with them old muskets." The Greys leave La Bahía in high spirits.

Captain Morris estimates that the Greys can make it to San Antonio de Béxar in five or six days on horseback. The horses and the weather, however, have different ideas. A norther begins blowing almost as soon as you leave the old fort, and the uniform that was so heavy in New Orleans suddenly seems very thin indeed. Along the march, you discover that the mustangs Captain Dimmitt provided are no less ornery than those from Victoria. They love to sidle up against a tree without warning—generally with the rider's leg between the horse and the tree. You learn to ride very low in the saddle whenever a tree branch is near. At any one time, in fact, a good percentage of the company is employed in chasing the mounts rather than riding them.

Thus progress is slower than Captain Morris expected, and the company is in considerable disorder, stretching out over a couple of miles by the end of each day. The captain constantly orders the company to close up ranks, but the continuing mishaps with the horses and the wild weather prevent anything like an orderly march. The last straw comes when it starts to pour down rain. Everyone is rapidly soaked with the ice-cold rain-water, driven by a strong north wind. Your teeth are chattering and you wrap your bedroll around you.

Connor, who has caught a bad cold be-sides having an injured shoulder, is fairly miserable. When he begins to shake with the ague, you ride ahead to get Captain Morris. Connor asks if there is any shelter that he can get to before nightfall, and the captain tells him that the company expects to reach the *rancho* of a friendly Tejano family late that night. Captain

Morris loans Connor his big bay mare—
not everyone is riding half-wild mustangs
—and gives him directions to the *rancho*.
The company continues to slog along as
Connor waves to you and rides ahead
through the driving rain.

When you arrive at the *rancho*, it is
after midnight and the rain has finally let
up. A couple of large fires are burning in
front of an adobe house. After they unsad-
dle their horses, the men crowd as close
as they dare to the heat of the fires. The
señora of the household passes out mugs
of steaming black coffee and sweet *choco-*

late. After you are fairly warm—if not yet dry—you go in to check on Connor.

He is not there. You want to go at once to look for him, but Captain Morris will not let you. It will be light within a few hours, he says, and a search party can look for him then.

"But he's sick!" you say. "He may have passed out and be lying out there on the trail. In that storm we could have ridden right by him."

But Captain Morris is not in the mood to argue about it. "Don't you worry about Connor, Tom," he says, "he probably took a wrong trail and is bivouacked somewhere. The rain has let up—he's tough, he'll be all right."

You are not so sure.

If you decide to disobey orders to go look for Connor, turn to page 35

If you decide to remain at the rancho for the night, turn to page 127

Even though General Cós still had a superior force in numbers, he surrendered when he found himself trapped in the Alamo—surrounded by Texan sharpshooters who were able to pick off his soldiers whenever they showed a head above the mission's crumbling walls. You wonder how Herman and Peter and Henry and the rest of the Greys fared in the battle. General Burleson received a promise from General Cós, according to the formal rules of warfare, that Cós would retire beyond the Río Grande, never to take up arms against Texas again. Noah just spat when he heard about the terms of the surrender. "Them rules of warfare aren't going to matter a whit to Santa Anna when he gets here. We'll see Cós in Texas again, you mark my words."

Other folks seemed to think the war was over—at least for a while. Many of the Texas volunteers in San Antonio left the army to go see about their farms and to spend Christmas with their families—even General Burleson himself. The most exciting news is that almost 200 men marched out of San Antonio on December 30 with Dr. James Grant, intent on carrying the war into Mexico by attacking Matamoros. Most of the Greys went on this expedition, including the Second

Company of Greys from New Orleans who signed up that same night at Bank's Arcade but traveled to Texas by ship across the Gulf.

Smithwick, pounding the hot iron on his anvil with unusual fury, has nothing but scorn for Dr. Grant, claiming that the shrewd Scot led the expedition into Mexico solely to regain possession of some estates there that were confiscated by the government. Of course, all this left San Antonio de Béxar in a very bad way. Right now, while Dr. Grant is marching on Matamoros, the Alamo is under the command of Colonel James C. Neill—with scarcely 100 men and very few arms or supplies. Grant not only drew off most of the men but commandeered every weapon worth taking in the city. Worst of all, rumor has it that General Santa Anna himself is about to cross the Río Grande with *thousands* of soldiers.

When Colonel Crockett hears all this, he is suddenly in quite a hurry to get on down to Béxar. Smithwick, however, tells him that it does not look like you will be able to make it. "There's still fever in his eyes," he says, "and there ain't nothing between here and Béxar 'cept Comanches. You better let the boy stay with me till he's fit enough to ride."

The fever was obviously as hard on Smithwick as it has been on you, but he seems to have been recuperating while shoeing horses, not while being tended by a kindly farmer's wife and daughter. You're not sure whether the fever is coming on again or not, but you badly want to rejoin the Greys. Herman will really take notice when you ride in with Crockett—if he has not gone off with Dr. Grant to invade Mexico. On the other hand, you remember how light-headed you felt riding across the prairie. Coming down with the fever again between here and San Antonio could cost you your life.

If you decide to go on with Crockett, turn to page 75

If you decide to stay in Bastrop for a few days, turn to page 115

In his headquarters in the long barracks, Travis is writing messages to be carried out. Sutherland, whose leg was broken when his horse fell on him coming back from the scouting mission, is headed for Gonzales. Another boy, just a bit older than you, is given a message for Fannin.

Davy Crockett, who has taken up the most dangerous position along the palisade between the church and the low barracks, takes you aside. "Thomas Benton," he says, "now I know you'd like nothing better than to stay here and practice up yore shooting eye on a passel of them Mexican soldiers, but I have an idea that things here are going to get mighty tight in just a little bit. Now I ain't saying you can't stay—you were man enough to ride in here under your own steam and I reckon you got the wherewithal to stick it out. My motto has always been to be sure you're right, and then go on ahead, but just personally, I'd be mighty pleased if you would run up to Buck Travis's office there and tell him I want you to take one of his letters wherever he wants it to go."

So this is it. You have a pretty good idea that if you stay in the Alamo, it will be the last thing you ever do. If you go to Travis, he will surely give you a message of some sort to take somewhere—the man loves to

102

write letters.

If you decide to stay in the Alamo, go on to the next page

If you decide to take a message for Travis, turn to page 143

It is not that you particularly want to die in this crumbling old mission on the edge of nowhere, but you feel deep inside that you somehow belong here. You think about your brother Robert and the others, back on the farm in Arkansas, and how you will probably never see them again. But even if you leave the Alamo to take a message somewhere for Travis, you will probably end up fighting these same Mexican soldiers with Fannin or maybe with Houston. Even if you survive all the battles, you know that it is not likely you will ever return to Arkansas. Then you think about your grandfather, how he risked everything to fight the British and win a new country, carving out a place for liberty in the world. Finally you think about why you came to Texas in the first place. If you hadn't come with the Greys to fight for the right all people should have—the right to a free and fair voice in their own governing—you would have come here for that very freedom.

You turn to Crockett and say, "Sir, I'm very much obliged for the offer to get me out of the Alamo, seeing as we're quite likely to die here, but I think stopping Santa Anna is about as important as anything I'm likely to do with the rest of my life. I am sure I'm right, so I guess I'll go ahead and stick around and see how things turn out."

"Private Thomas Benton," Crockett says solemnly, "I shore do wish you'd been born in Tennessee." Going over to the bundle of buckskins and blankets that are his belongings, Crockett pulls out a well-worn coonskin hat. "Here, boy, I'd like you to wear this."

It is without doubt the proudest moment of your life.

By late that afternoon the gates of the Alamo have closed upon as determined a group of freedom-loving frontiersmen as ever looked down the barrel of a Kentucky rifle. The enemy troops can be seen scurrying about, taking up their positions. At the Veramendi house soldiers are building a mount for a five-inch howitzer; earthworks are appearing nearer and nearer the walls. From the bell tower of San Fernando cathedral, some 800 yards away, a huge red banner unfurls, signifying that there will be no quarter for the Texans and Tejanos inside the Alamo. Travis sends out his orderly, Albert Martin, to talk with the representative of the Mexican forces, Colonel Almonte, under a white flag on the footbridge over the river by Potrero Street. But Martin returns in less than an hour to confirm the message of the red banner: only unconditional surrender will be accepted—otherwise, all the defenders will be put to the sword. Travis answers the offer by touching off the eighteen-pounder.

"I reckon that means the war is on," says Crockett. He picks up old Betsy, his favorite hunting rifle, and calmly looks out over the wall. You follow his gaze to where a Mexican soldier appears briefly at the edge of some trees about 150 yards off. When he appears again a few moments later, the two-part explosion of the Kentucky flintlock breaks the evening silence. The soldier drops like a squirrel out of a tree. Cheers erupt for Crockett's marksmanship. A short while later James Bonham can be seen whipping his dun horse and hanging low in the saddle, riding hard toward the main gate of the Alamo. Once inside, he reports to Travis. Fannin will remain at Goliad.

Late that night Gregorio Esparza, one of Captain Juan Seguín's best scouts and an expert with artillery, is the last one into the fort. His family remained in town until the very last minute, gleaning as much information from the Mexican soldiers as possible before making their final retreat into the Alamo. One by one, they are hauled into the fort on a rope. With the little Spanish you have learned and the little English Gregorio's son Enrique knows, you talk about the Mexican army as you help get the family settled. Just a little younger than you are, Enrique is impressed that you are a *soldado*. You in turn, are impressed that he has proved such a successful spy for the Tejanos. Finally you turn in, sleeping rolled up in your buffalo hide next to the Tennesseans' campfire. It is the end of the first day of the siege.

The next day, February 24, Jim Bowie's mysterious illness takes a final turn for the worse, rendering him incapable of getting out of bed, much less of commanding the volunteers. You remember that even Crockett was a little awed by the man and his knife. Holding the foot-long blade in his hands, Crockett remarked that just seeing it was "enough to give a man of squeamish stomach the colic, especially before breakfast!" If Bowie, confined to his cot, is ever to use the famous weapon again, it will indeed be at close quarters. With little fanfare, Travis becomes the garrison's sole commander.

That night, Travis writes the best letter of his life:

COMMANDANCY OF THE ALAMO

February 24th, 1836

*To the People of Texas & All
Americans in the World.*

*Fellow Citizens & Compatriots I am
besieged, by a thousand or more of
the Mexicans under Santa Anna – I
have sustained a continual Bombardment & cannonade for 24
hours & have not lost a man – The
enemy has demanded a surrender
at discretion, otherwise, the garrison are to be put to the sword, if the
fort is taken – I have answered the
demand with a cannon shot, & our
flag still waves proudly from the
walls – I shall never surrender or
retreat. Then, I call on you in the
name of Liberty, of patriotism &
everything dear to the American
character, to come to our aid, with
all dispatch – The enemy is receiv-
ing reinforcements daily & will no
doubt increase to three or four thousand in four or five days. If this call
is neglected, I am determined to
sustain myself as long as possible*

& die like a soldier who never forgets what is due to his own honor
& that of his country—VICTORY
OR DEATH.
>   William Barret Travis
>   Lt. Col. Comdt.

•   •   •

The unerring marksmanship of the Alamo defenders plays a large part over the
next few days in keeping Santa Anna's
forces away from the walls, but there is
little to be done about the increasing cannon bombardment—except to find a safe
place and keep your head covered. Occasionally the defenders return the cannon
fire, but generally only when a Mexican
cannonball is recovered—sometimes they
just bounce across the plaza. The scrap
iron Sam Blair collected will be effective
against the ranks of the attackers, but is
useless when it comes to aiming at the
Mexican cannon emplacements.

Time passes as if there is no night and
no day. The overcast skies reflect the
continuous cannon blasts and the thousands of campfires around the fort; Santa
Anna orders his brass band to play in the
middle of the night, for the sole purpose
of disrupting the sleep of the Alamo
defenders. As if the noise and martial

music are not enough, another norther howls in, dropping the temperature into the teens. It is a dry, blistering sort of cold that brings tears to the eyes whenever you try to aim.

Travis sends James Bonham out once again to try and convince Fannin to come to the aid of the Alamo, but he worries that his messengers are not getting through. On Sunday, February 28, Travis asks Captain Juan Seguín, a native of San Antonio and the much respected captain of the Tejanos in the Alamo, to try and sneak through the Mexican lines, pretending to be a Mexican *ranchero*. Seguín goes at once to borrow Jim Bowie's horse, the best in the fort. Bowie, an old friend of the Seguín family, is so sick that he barely recognizes Juan. Finally he comes around, and tells him, "*Sí,* take my horse. *Vaya con Dios.*" Before dawn on February 29, Seguín and two of his men, Antonio Cruz y Arocha and Alejandro de la Garza, calmy saunter into the dark.

But even if the days merge into one another, significant events continue. On March 1 Sutherland and Smith's ride to Gonzales bears fruit when thirty-two men under John Smith and George Kimball slip through the Mexican lines, only to be challenged by the Alamo sentry—who actually shoots one of the volunteers in the foot before Smith can make himself known. On March 2 Bonham rides like a fury through a hail of Mexican bullets, returning from Goliad for the last time. He made the round trip in less than four days, and, as he dismounts, his horse falls dead at his feet.

"Jim," says Travis, embracing him, "You didn't have to come back."

Bonham replies, "Buck, I couldn't leave you in this mess alone. Victory or death, you know." The two men have been friends since their childhood days in South Carolina, where they doted on stories of the American revolutionary hero, the Swamp Fox. "Victory or Death" was also the motto of that hero, who borrowed it from another southerner, Patrick Henry.

Remarkably, there are no casualties in the Alamo. A few men have been injured by flying rocks from the cannon blasts, but not one man has been killed. Every so often a company of Mexican soldiers approaches the walls, hiding behind what little cover Travis has left unburned beyond the walls, crouching and crawling their way toward the fort until, at about 100 yards, the Alamo cannon belch out a deadly scattering of nails, pieces of horse-

shoes, and other scrap. Then the defenders, almost casually and often with Crockett singing out "Come to My Bower" in the background, lean their long rifles out over the top of the wall and take a wicked toll on anything that moves.

Crockett's style is impressive. One day a Mexican engineer is walking openly along the river about 200 yards away, well out of anyone's range. Crockett, his long hair flowing and his buckskin fringe blowing, calmly stands up on top of the wall, licks his thumb to test the wind, raises his rifle a little higher than usual, and—with Mexican bullets flying all around him—shoots the engineer dead. It gets so that whenever Crockett stands up (he seems to be recognizable at any distance) every Mexican soldier in sight hits the ground. Still, Crockett does not like to be penned up, and he says several times that he would like to make a direct assault on the Mexicans. "If I could jest draw a bead on old Santa Anna, we could have these fellers on the run in no time." You agree with the idea, but the thought of actually going out among the thousands of enemy soldiers is terrifying.

When he is not encouraging the men on the walls with his tall tales and singing and fiddling—or his incredible marksmanship—Crockett plays with the several children in the Alamo. Antony Wolfe's two sons are especially fond of Crockett's stories and silly songs, and they pull on the tail of his coonskin hat when he pretends not to look. You take it as the greatest compliment in the world that he treats you like a real soldier and not like a child.

Turn to page 137

The "few days" in Bastrop with Noah ends up being closer to a couple of months. No one else comes through town headed for Béxar because everyone is headed for Gonzales to join Houston's army there. Both you and Noah recover from the fever as winter wanes. Noah, meanwhile, joins up with a company of Rangers to try and put down a Comanche uprising before it gets out of hand. He is gone most of February while you run the blacksmith shop in Bastrop. Noah succeeded in teaching you the basics of horseshoeing before he left, so while he is gone you shoe horses. You are sure, however, that your life in Texas after shoeing horses will be dangerous. If anyone riding a horse with some of those first sets of shoes you put on ever sees you again, he may be inclined to shoot you. Pretty bad, if you say so yourself.

Around March 1 families from all over the countryside begin gathering at Bastrop. News is spreading like wildfire that Santa Anna has the Alamo surrounded by thousands of troops and that he intends to exterminate the Anglos in Texas. This is small comfort to the native Tejanos, for Santa Anna has left little in the wake of his armies so far to prove his goodwill toward anyone. Soon the road out of Bastrop is jammed with families fleeing east toward San Felipe, like every other road out of South Texas. People are calling it the Runaway Scrape, meaning that people are scraping up what belongings they can carry and running away. When the news comes that the Alamo has fallen, the exodus becomes a general evacuation—the entire population of South Texas seems to be on the road ahead of Santa Anna's advancing armies. Every available male, however, heads for Gonzales, where Houston is still building up his army. While waiting for news of Noah, you learn that General Gaona is headed directly for Bastrop—and that General Sesma is on the road to Gonzales, closely followed by Santa Anna himself.

All this time you had imagined that General Houston must have been fortifying Gonzales, but it turns out that the little town on the Guadalupe River was merely a gathering point. Noah finally appears to help with the evacuation of Bastrop—the Indians have been forgotten while there is the greater danger from the invading armies. He tells you that Houston is evacuating Gonzales and heading east. You decide to go on without Noah, who will remain as a rear-guard scout until the Mexican army under General

Gaona appears. The Colorado River is running strong, so you take a canoe with a few provisions and head downstream. If you are lucky, you can catch up with Houston at Burnham's Crossing when the army has to cross the Colorado. You say good-bye to Noah and turn your canoe into the current.

The trip downriver is uneventful, lasting only three and a half days. Reaching Burnham's Crossing on March 18, you find a horde of settlers in the process of crossing the Colorado. Encamped nearby is Houston himself and the army—a mere 400 men.

Turn to page 163

You have time to think back now on all that just happened. Six months ago you were just an Arkansas farmboy who had never used a rifle on anything bigger than a squirrel. It seems so long ago. Then you think about all the young men, the noble young warriors of the New Orleans Greys, who came together from a dozen different states, from different countries even, that one night in New Orleans to pledge their lives for the sake of liberty in this land called Texas. Some died at the Siege of Béxar, some at the Alamo; some died under Urrea's lances at San Patricio; some died gallantly fighting at the Battle of Coleto; many were slaughtered outside the walls of La Bahia. So many brave men! You wonder if you and Herman are the last living members of the New Orleans Greys. Herman is thinking along the same lines as you trudge north.

"This is going to be a story," he says, "that will be told with those of the Spartans at Thermopylae, of the Maccabees, of Boadicea at London, of Roland at Roncesvalles."

You do not have any idea what he is talking about, but you say, "I guess that makes us famous?"

"Not us, exactly. But those men who

stayed in the Alamo will never be forgotten, not as long as people care about their freedom. But I intend to make sure that no one forgets the New Orleans Greys either."

"You going to write a book about us?" you ask. "I've seen you scribbling away in your diary all along."

"Alas, my poor diary," moans Herman. "I am afraid that in our haste to get across the Rio San Antonio back there, my diary decided to take that path to swim to the sea."

"You dropped it in the river? Oh no," you say. "That's terrible."

"Fortunately, Tom, I have an excellent memory. I have no doubt that I will be able to recall everything that happened on this campaign—and every word that was spoken."

"If you can remember all the speeches we've heard on this trip," you say, "you've got a better head for it than I do."

Only a day or two ahead of Urrea's forces to begin with, you start seeing his scouts and cavalry outriders on a daily basis. That is when you come upon a small farm just outside of Victoria. Two horses, hungry but otherwise in pretty good shape, have returned to the farm after it was abandoned—which appears to have happened in the last day or so. It is an eerie sight. Food is still on the table, with some unwashed dishes; clothes lie in a heap next to some neatly folded, as if the job had been interrupted and never resumed.

You catch the horses and bridle them, but must ride bareback since there are no saddles to be found. Just as you leave the little farm, shots ring out. You've been seen by some of Urrea's scouts. You ride hell for leather into Victoria, which is just as empty of inhabitants as the farm. You swim the horses across the Guadalupe, then ride to the top of a small rise where you stop to take stock of the situation.

Below you can see a party of eight or ten Mexican soldiers just beginning to urge their horses into the river. With no guns, with Herman's sword cut beginning to fester and your arm just starting to heal from the gunshot, and with only open country before you, things do not look good at all.

"We've got to warn the army that Urrea is coming this way," Herman says. "And tell them about the massacre at Goliad."

"Which way do we go?" you ask. "Surely they are not still at Gonzales. Do you think Houston would try to fight Santa Anna there?"

"No, I don't think he has enough men to fight it out on the open prairie against a trained army. But there aren't any forts like the Alamo or La Bahía east of Gonzales."

"Maybe he will try to lure them down into the bayou country," you suggest. "Or he could be taking the army up to San Felipe de Austin."

"That Mexican party is almost across," says Herman. "We've got to hurry up. Which way do we go? Maybe we'd better split up."

"That's probably best—that way at least one of us may get through to Houston. I'll head straight north of San Felipe."

"Good," says Herman. "I'll take the

coast road up through Matagorda and Brazoria. Farewell!"

Just then the Mexicans begin firing as they ride up out of the river. "Farewell! Remember to put me in your book!" you yell as you turn your horse north and kick him to a fast gallop. Hanging on Indian-style with both hands around the horse's neck, you lean as far to one side as you can manage. When the Mexican soldiers top the hill were you parted from Herman, the bullets began flying like hail. By the time the soldiers decide which of you they will follow, you are safely out of range. You race past a small grove of trees and then down a dry creek bed.

Heading due north across the absolute-

ly empty plains and low hills that lie between the Guadalupe and the Colorado, you know that you will come to Beason's Crossing. You can cross the Colorado there and then catch the road east to San Felipe; at the least, you can get news at the ferry about where Houston has taken the army. Seventy-five miles and three days later, you arrive at the crossing— only to find General Joaquín de Ramírez y Sesma and his army of 725 soldiers, just completing their crossing. The Colorado, swollen with rain for several days, apparently held up Sesma's advance toward San Felipe, only twenty-five miles away. You figure that Houston must be ahead of them, so you turn your horse east and follow the river a few miles until you find another spot to cross.

Wet, without a rifle, and with a very tired horse, you are helped up the east bank of the river by a silent, gaunt man of about 50 dressed in well-worn buckskins. His bright blue eyes are deeply set in a weathered face. This is Sam Houston's chief scout, Deaf Smith. "Saw you at the crossing," Smith says. "Followed you downriver."

You immediately adopt his silent ways—he is not really deaf, just an excellent spy. You follow him into the woods.

After he hears all the news you have, most of which he knows already, he tells you that Houston and the army are up the Brazos from San Felipe at Groce's Ferry, where he is drilling the army. Santa Anna, he says, is only a few miles behind General Sesma. Smith advises you to follow the Colorado, now that you have crossed, back to Beason's Crossing, wait until Sesma's troops are well past, then slip into the wooded hills across the road before Santa Anna's army appears. From there you are to head northeast for twenty miles to Groce's Ferry.

It is pretty rough going. Slipping between two armies was easy compared to making your way through the trackless thicket you find yourself in now. You end up leading your horse most of the twenty miles to the ferry. You arrive on April 13, just in time to join the army in crossing the Brazos on the steamboat *Yellowstone*. You deliver your news directly to Houston, a huge man who is dressed half in military garb, half in Cherokee buckskins. When you are through relating your story, he calls over General Burleson, who is commanding the infantry.

"This is Tom Benton," Houston says to the general, "one tough young buck who says he served under you at Béxar."

"Didn't know we had any young'uns at the siege, Sam, but if he's got this far, I reckon he must be tough as an old boot. I'll see if the quartermaster can't round him up a rifle."

Herman, if he survived, has not yet arrived. You follow General Burleson to get fitted out.

Turn to page 165

The next morning two search parties ride out at dawn to look for Connor. At the point where the path to the *rancho* breaks off from the main road to Bexar, you realize that Connor must simply have missed the turning in the dark and gone on down the main track. No one thinks anything serious could have happened to him, so you look for the smoke of a campfire.

You find no campfires, however. About two miles up the road you find Connor under a tree, wrapped up in his blanket, as still as a stone. But Connor did not die of exposure. There are three bullet holes in his chest—and two deep bayonet wounds. His rifle and boots are gone. One of the older men, an experienced hunter, finds marks across the road indicating that another man was wounded—or killed—and dragged away. Further on you find a Mexican soldier's cap. Connor did not go down without a fight. Tears fill your eyes, and you curse Captain Morris for not letting you come look for Connor last night.

"Laddie," says the old hunter, "those Mexicans were obviously waiting to ambush any one of us coming down this road. If you'd 'a come out after Connor last night, you'd be lying right there beside him now."

The weather dries out, and the horses seem to settle down a bit. In a scant two days you reach San Antonio. It is November 21. After you make sure that Connor will get a Christian burial in a local Catholic cemetery, you sleep for almost twenty-four hours. The following day, the twin company of New Orleans Greys under Captain Breeze arrives. They left New Orleans three days before you, coming overland through Nacogdoches. There is a good deal of merrymaking among the men, all of whom had signed up to fight for Texas on the same night back at Bank's Arcade.

You spend the next few days getting to know the camp. Among the newly arrived Greys you meet three young Germans—Herman Ehrenberg, Peter Mattern, and Henry Curtman. Herman, at 18, is the youngest. Like you, he is a runaway—though he ran away from college and his father in Germany instead of a small dirt farm in Arkansas. Still, you have some things in common, and he takes to you at once. Like poor Connor, Herman has a taste for wine and a yen for the company of pretty señoritas. There is very little wine in Béxar, but the *ron blanco* runs freely and the señoritas of San Antonio are rumored to be the prettiest anywhere. Of course, both will have to wait until the Mexican forces have been driven out of the city. As Herman puts it, "I cannot wait to be a 'liberating soldier.' Women are supposed to love liberating soldiers."

"You read too many stories, my friend," puts in Peter Mattern. "You have to liberate them from dragons for that—not dragoons."

Go on to the next page

The Greys are far and away the most organized company in the Texas Army. You are all dressed in clothing of the same color—if not always of the same cut or style—and you are all armed with roughly the same weapons; the Greys camp as a single group and share camp duties. The Texas volunteers, however, form about as diverse an assortment of humanity as can be imagined. Scouts, hunters, farmers— whole families in some cases. Men dress in buckskins—some fresh and yellow, some black with grease—some wear jeans, some oddly formal bits and pieces of U.S. military uniforms; there are boots, brogans, and moccasins; stovepipe hats and beaver hats, coonskin hats and straw hats, broad sombreros and military caps, feathered Indian headbands and no hats at all; the weaponry encompasses just about every sort of firearm made in the past thirty years.

The camp is a scattered affair, but generally centered around an old grist mill about a mile and a quarter north-northwest of the main plaza of San Antonio de Béxar, a mile due north of the Alamo mission-turned-fortress where General Cós is headquartered. The cottonwood trees (*alamos*) so common along most of the river are strangely absent near the fortress, having been cut to allow for a clear field of fire from the walls. The Alamo sits in isolation from the rest of the town, easily visible for a half-mile in any direction. The first few days you and Herman and the others spend at a small entrenchment thrown up by Cooke's men where two small six-pounder cannon are mounted. To get to the cannon emplacement you have to cross some 600 yards of flat open space—what was once a cornfield. Cós's cannoneers rake the field with grapeshot whenever anyone starts across, so you have to run like the wind to a large pecan tree in the middle of the field. You line up in a single file behind it while the Mexican cannoneers blast away at the tree limbs above and the field around you, then you dash the rest of the way while they reload. It is a lot of fun, though dangerous.

Once at the cannon emplacement, you take turns loading, aiming, and firing the two cannon, cheering whenever a shot hits the Alamo walls. Not a little betting goes on—mostly musket balls, money being in rather short supply all around. In the evenings, the dull task of melting lead and casting it into bullets is less tiresome because almost everyone involved is making bullets for someone else to pay debts piled up because of poor marksmanship with the cannon. You, to your own surprise, turn out to be a fair shot with the cannon. Herman, casting the last of the 100 bullets he owes you, says, "Tom, I sure am glad I didn't bet you cannonballs.

The cannoneer everyone marvels at, however, is a tall gangly backwoodsman in a pea-green coat named Deaf Smith. Already a legendary scout and Indian fighter, Deaf Smith can target and hit the individual windows in the Alamo barracks wall using the little six-pounder at roughly 600 yards.

Meanwhile, the Texan leaders are making plans. The Battle of Concepción gave the Texans an idea of just how effective frontier fighting techniques can be against a regular army. The only word for it is devastating. General Burleson, however, feels that the month-long siege has not weakened Cós at all and that a successful assault on the town is impossible. Burleson goes so far as to order a tactical retreat to Gonzales for the rest of the winter.

Colonel Johnson, Major Morris, and old Ben Milam (No one ever calls Milam "colonel," though he is one.) disagree with this policy. One day a Mexican deserter comes into camp. Interrogated in front of a number of the men, the deserter brings news that spreads through the camp like wildfire – the Mexican army is running low on food and is disheartened by the growing number of volunteers flocking to the Texas Army. You take that to mean the Greys in particular.

But General Burleson refuses to rescind his orders. After a lengthy argument, Milam bursts from the headquarters tent. "Who will go with old Ben Milam into San Antonio?" he roars out. A chorus of cheers goes up. "Then fall in line!" This is what you've been waiting for. Within minutes you and some 240 other men, including every one of the Greys, have volunteered to invade San Antonio. It is December 4.

Burleson has to agree to the invasion. The troops are ordered to take a long siesta while the plans are worked out. By midnight the invasion is under way. Burleson holds most of the army in reserve on the edge of town. Colonel Johnson positions his battalion at the northern end of the Calle de Soledad. Ben Milam leads his to the head of the Calle de Acéquia, which runs parallel to Soledad. At three in the morning Colonel J. C. Neill opens up on

the Alamo with the two six-pounders you know so well.

Turn to page 173

The next few days are little short of terrifying. A long column of Mexican soldiers appears—well over 1,000, including the crack *zapadores* unit—marching into San Antonio under General Gaona. General Cós is also back in town, with revenge uppermost in his mind. To the southeast, on Powder House Hill, yet another bloodred flag is raised. At midnight on Thursday, March 3, Travis hands his latest packet of messages to John Smith. Other men are scribbling messages to their families on whatever scraps of paper can be found. No one doubts that this is the last chance to communicate with his loved ones. You, too, put in a few words to Robert back in Arkansas.

Once again, Travis has waxed eloquent, this time in a letter to the Texas leaders meeting at Washington-on-the-Brazos:

Let the Convention go on and make a declaration of independence, and we will then understand, and the world will understand, what we are fighting for. If independence is not declared, I shall lay down my arms, and so will the men under my command. But under the flag of independence, we are ready to peril our lives a hundred times a day. . . ."

Smith leaves the fort in the dead of night, his saddle bags stuffed with letters, silently working his way east. On the northern side of the Alamo you join a number of Texans who move out beyond the walls and begin firing at random. The diversion works—soon Mexican soldiers are swarming toward the northern postern. Their white pants seem to glow in the dark, making them easy targets. Load and fire, quickly crawl a few feet down the trench, load and fire, over and over again. Monotonous almost—until you look up to see a Mexican soldier bearing down on you. You haven't reloaded, so you draw your brother's big dirk and thrust at the man, who topples onto you, his bayonet slashing the back of your calf. But he is already dead, shot between the eyes by someone a few yards away. Splattered with the soldier's brains and blood, your leg burning with the cut, you roll the man off you, and begin limping back to the gate. You cannot get the soldier's face out of your mind.

On the morning of March 4 you and everyone else suddenly discover that the old mission walls are not so sturdy as was believed. Santa Anna has moved his cannon batteries on the north, up to within 250 yards. Across the river to the west

two twin nine-pounders hit the same section of wall all day. Jameson has you continuously digging trenches across the plaza. The dirt is used to support the western wall, which is now shaking visibly with each hit. Explosive shells repeatedly fall within the walls, showering you with rocks and dirt. The weather has suddenly turned warmer, adding to the discomfort of the already hot and dirty job. Your leg throbs from the bayonet wound. You are incredibly tired that night, but sleep comes only in short fits, broken time and again by bugles and incoming artillery. The next morning finds the northern cannon within 200 yards. You spend the day trying to pick off the cannoneers, though only Crockett and a few other marksmen are even occasionally effective at that range. By early evening, the cannonade tapers off, replaced by an eerie quiet.

Travis, you suspect, has an idea of what is coming. About 5 P.M. he calls for a general assembly, leaving only a few sentries on the walls. There is no hope, Travis tells the men bluntly, of any help coming in time now. Tomorrow you will face a major assault, Travis feels sure, and now is the time for anyone to leave who is not committed to the cause of freedom. "Our role here is to delay Santa Anna as long as possible, to make any victory he may win in this place cost him more dearly than he imagines possible."

By staying, you will buy time for General Houston to prepare a larger Texas force to attack the Mexican armies. To leave now, however, may mean that you can join Houston and fight again. One older man, a Frenchman named Louis Rose who fought in several European wars, has not shown himself to be a coward at all during the siege. But he says in no uncertain terms that to stay is madness: "I fight to live, not to die." Later that night he slips over the wall.

You are so young—just a boy—that several of the men urge you to go. You have done enough, they tell you. Just slip into the river, they say, and you can almost swim out of town. No one will blame you.

If you decide to stay in the Alamo, turn to page 147

If you decide to escape and try to join Houston, turn to page 61

You do not want to leave Crockett and the few New Orleans Greys left in the Alamo, but there is no choice about it when Travis leans out of his doorway and yells, "Colonel Crockett, can you spare your young'un there? The Mexicans won't believe he is a messenger even if they catch him trying to slip out of town."

"Yep, Buck, I was just trying to talk him into that very job," says Crockett. "Go on, Tom. It's a job worth doing just as much as the fighting is."

Travis gives you a packet of letters addressed to Houston and some other Texas leaders who may still be in Gonzales. If Houston has left Gonzales, you are to follow him as quickly as possible. Travis orders a mount for you, which turns out to be a half-wild little pony. Since Sutherland just left for Gonzales a short while ago, you wonder what more Travis could have to say. Still, as Crockett says, it is a job worth doing, and getting through the Mexican lines will not be an easy task. Toward midnight you walk the pony out the main gate. You turn left and walk past the palisade. Crockett leans over to bid you farewell. "Tom Benton," he says, "you tell old General Sam that Davy Crockett says for him to get himself down here in a hurry."

"I will, Colonel Crockett," you reply.

"And Tom, be careful."

Getting out of Béxar proves to be no problem. There are still large gaps in the Mexican lines. You can see, however, that more troops are arriving even now, in the middle of the night. The road south to Laredo must be one long string of Mexican soldiers, you think, all coming to besiege this tiny fort. Heading north, you follow the Alamo *acéquia* until it approaches the river again. There are more Mexican troops camped along the river. You turn east and walk the pony until it is light enough to ride. Once you come to the Gonzales road, you must ride past the refugees from Béxar. Trotting among the creaking, overloaded ox carts, the women with packs on their backs and bundles on their heads, the old men pushing hand trucks, the knots of children and family groups, you gallop along the clear stretches of the road. You reach Gonzales in three days.

Houston, however, is not at Gonzales. He is at Washington-on-the-Brazos, attending the convention there that is busy declaring Texas an independent republic. You ride on, headed for the Brazos. By the time you get there, Houston is just preparing to return to Gonzales. You deliver the messages, but they only sadden him. "Those brave men down in Béxar are buying us time," he tells the convention. "Pray for their souls, gentlemen, for they will surely perish. And pray that they buy us enough time to prepare for what is coming."

You return with the Old General, as they call him, though it takes everything your little pony is capable of to keep up with Houston's big white charger Saracen. With his Cherokee coat and buckskin vest, silver spurs with huge rowels, broad hat with a feather in the brim, and sideburns that puff out two inches on each side of his face, Sam Houston is a sight to see. Not to mention that he is nearly six feet, six inches tall. When the road is smooth, he pulls out a beat-up copy of *Gulliver's Travels* and reads while he rides. He is the most unusual soldier you have ever met, but at the same time you know that, as quietly as his commands are issued, no one would dare disobey them.

Turn to page 195

After the assembly breaks up, everyone returns to his post. Crockett and his Tennesseans pass around the last jug of corn whiskey in the fort while they smoke an assortment of pipes and cigars. The quiet persists all night. After twelve days of continual cannonade, the quiet is deafening. Even the sentries nod and doze. Finally, there is only one man awake in the entire compound. Captain John Baugh is startled by wild bugling just before dawn. There was no sound from his watches posted outside the wall. They were already dead. By the time you are almost awake, Baugh is halfway across the plaza, shouting "Colonel Travis! Colonel Travis! The Mexicans are coming!" In no time at all, the garrison is on the walls, guns blazing at the seemingly endless columns of advancing soldiers. You know this is it—this time the Mexicans are dragging ladders and carrying long pikes.

After the first few rounds are fired, Crockett orders you down off the walls. For an hour or more you load rifles one after another for the Tennesseans. Across the plaza you hear Travis call out to Seguín's company, "*No rendirse, muchachos!*" Manning the northern cannon, Travis leans briefly over the wall to fire his shotgun point-blank at the Mexicans already scaling the wall. You see him straighten suddenly, grasp his head, then roll down the cannon ramp, dead. He never even drew his sword. You see 16-year-old Galba Fuqua stumble into the chapel, bleeding profusely from a bullet-shattered jaw. During the odd, seconds-long lulls that occur without explanation, you can hear the cries of Angelina Dickinson, the colonel's baby daughter, from inside the chapel sacristy. Almost above their heads, Dickinson's and Bonham's cannon shake the church with thunder. They are as deadly with cannon as they are with rifles — thirty or forty men fall every time the guns spew their scrap metal loads.

The first attack repulsed, you have time to climb the palisade again. Crockett and his men have proved that what appears to be the fort's weakest point is anything but. For 100 yards in front of the palisade, the ground is literally covered with Mexican dead. Crockett looks out over the wall, commenting, "You've got to give 'em credit. There's a whole lot of brave soldiers lying out yonder."

You see the ranks re-forming and the cannonade begins again. The north wall is crumbling. Again you load rifles one after another. There are bugle calls on every side. The defenders atop the walls are thinning out, having to cover more and more space as their comrades fall. Finally the Mexicans retreat once more.

Santa Anna's brass is repeating over and over the Deguello, the Mexican battle march which signals fire and death only, with no surrender and no prisoners. In the short lulls Crockett plays his fiddle and sings at the top of his lungs. John McGregor, the Scot who helped you saw so many boards, puffs his bagpipes—making fighting music every bit as fierce as Santa Anna's trumpets, but it is somehow joyous at the same time. Crockett says the Deguello is the meanest, most bloodcurdling music ever invented, and that he'd like to ram a bugle down the throat of the man who wrote it.

Finally a third assault begins. Endless streams of Mexican soldiers rush the walls, frightened as much by the human mass behind them as by the guns before them. Crockett is still hurling insults when you see Mexican soldiers coming over the north wall, quickly followed by more on the west. Dickinson's cannon rakes the plaza from atop the church as a tide of soldiers sweeps toward you. Bullets are everywhere. There is no more loading to be done—you have used the last of the powder. Above you the Tennesseans are using their rifles as deadly clubs, smashing skulls and collarbones, slashing and stabbing with dirks and Bowie knives, leaving the palisade covered with blood and bodies.

With Travis and most of the other officers dead or pinned down elsewhere around the plaza, John Baugh takes command, signaling the defenders into the barracks. The last stand is planned for the two barracks buildings. Each doorway is fronted by parapets made of earth packed inside stretched buffalo hides. What is left of the Alamo garrison slowly retreats across the plaza, giving ground yard by yard, foot by foot, finally taking up positions behind the buffalo-hide parapets. In the low barracks, in a small room by the main gate, Jim Bowie waits impatiently for someone to open his door. Beside him are a brace of pistols and, of course, the knife.

The last few defenders jam into the small isolated barracks rooms, barricading the doors behind them. Once inside they begin firing through small windows and gun ports into the plaza. The Mexicans turn the Alamo's own eighteen-pounder around and begin firing from the northern wall into the barracks. One by one, the rooms literally explode inward. The cannon blows the heavy oaken doors of the church off their hinges. Mexican soldiers rush past you into the church, despite your best efforts. In fact, your rifle breaks in two over the head of one soldier, leaving you with only the barrel in your hands. Inside, Antony Wolfe's two sons run out of a side room and are bayoneted and tossed aside. You wonder if all the children of the Alamo will meet the same fate. Enrique Esparza is only slightly younger than you. You hope his Spanish will keep him safe—that he can talk his way out of being shot.

In front of you Crockett is still swinging old Betsy, laying out anyone approaching. He seems impervious to bullets, but finally staggers. A Mexican officer jumps down on him from a scaffold, wounding him badly in the head with a saber cut. In an instant Crockett is pinned to the ground by twenty or more bayonets. Standing with your back to one of the carved pillars in front of the church, your rifle broken and only your brother Robert's dirk in your hand, you feel a searing pain in your side, followed by another in your chest. Lying in front of the church, you see Robert Evans heading for the

powder magazine with a torch, but he is shot down before he can touch off the powder. Above you the Alamo cannon are finally silenced, and you know that both Enrique Esparza and Angelina Dickinson are now fatherless. The last thing you see, even as your eyes cloud over, is a Mexican officer hauling down the blue silk banner of the New Orleans Greys, that symbol of "God and Liberty," the last flag left flying over the Alamo. Less than five hours after the battle began, by 9 A.M., 183 Texans and Tejanos lie dead in the Alamo. Santa Anna's finest battalion of shock troops lost 670 men of its total contingent of 800. In all, some 1,600 Mexican soldiers lie dead, and another 500 are seriously wounded. After Santa Anna's departure, Francisco Ruiz, the *alcalde* of San Antonio de Béxar, has to order the Mexican dead thrown into the river—there is neither manpower nor cemetery space to bury them all. The ashes of the Alamo defenders, burned in a great pyre by Santa Anna, are buried together in a single mass grave.

The prospect of an actual battle is so much more exciting than lying around Smithwick's forge "getting well" that you insist on going to Béxar with the Greys. It is indeed a rough ride, but it would have been even without this off-and-on fever. Four days later you camp for the night in a green, moss-hung glade by a stream just a few miles north of Béxar. At least you think you are north of Béxar. To the west a mass of dark clouds is building on the horizon, which some men say is just another fast-moving storm, but others maintain must be smoke from Béxar. General Cós must be burning the city, they say. At any rate, you settle in for an evening of roast venison and delicious fresh hot coffee—the cook takes special pride in his coffee and making it is almost a ritual. To the west the sunset is an unusual bloodred.

In the middle of the night, however, you are awakened to a great howling out on the prairie. Two packs of wolves hurtle past the camp. Hundreds of coyotes follow, yapping and leaping. Suddenly the horses are all stamping and pawing the ground, pulling against the picket lines. Everyone is awake now, primarily concerned with keeping the horses from stampeding. Finally it sweeps into view—

a long line of red light flickering on the horizon. Within minutes the prairie fire is upon you, crackling and roaring, pushing waves of intense heat before it—until it is past. The four-foot-high dry winter grass of the prairie burns so quickly that the flames have come and gone before the dew-drenched bushes and trees along the little stream where you are camped have time to catch fire. All that is left when the sun finally rises is a black ocean of smoldering prairie. For most of this day's march you must wear a bandana over your face because of the blowing ash.

Closer to San Antonio the land again becomes green as the hills rise, covered with brush, dense mesquite thickets and small woods of cedar, oak, and pecan trees. Whether or not the fire drove them south, the land here is teeming with game—herds of deer, wild turkeys, trees full of birds. Approaching the city from the north, you are met by two guides, one American and one Tejano, who lead you to the Texas Army on the banks of the Río San Antonio. There you find the twin company of New Orleans Greys—arrived only two days before—who signed up that same night at Bank's Arcade, but came to Texas by ship over the Gulf. There are

many reunions this night and a great deal
of merrymaking.

Turn to page 131

Having proved to yourselves, to the Mexican army, and to everyone in Texas that the New Orleans Greys are a fighting force to be reckoned with, you find the march south enjoyable. It is all very heroic, and all along the way plans are made about what you will do to the Mexican soldiers in Matamoros—and what you will do with the Mexican silver, the señoritas, the glory. You can practically hear the songs being written about your heroic liberating invasion of Mexico.

The first stop is at Goliad, where Johnson and Grant "requisition" all of Captain Dimmitt's horses, much to the good captain's dismay. From there, you march to Refugio, where Fannin has assembled more volunteers, most newly arrived from the United States. They are all envious of the battle record of the Greys. They tell you that the story of the Siege of Béxar has already been reported in newspapers all over the country. You have no doubt at all that you are doing the right thing by invading Mexico—the difference between defending Texas and attacking Mexico is lost for the moment. But suddenly everything is in an uproar. The tallest man you have ever seen, General Sam Houston, commander-in-chief of all Texas forces, has called for a meeting of all the volunteers in Refugio. At the gathering Houston addresses the crowd:

> ... so great are my hopes that I firmly believe next summer I shall see the flag of Texas floating over all the harbors of our coast! But in order to win, we must act together. United we stand, divided we fall! I am told that you intend to take Matamoros; I praise your courage, but I will frankly confess to you, my friends, that I do not approve of your plans. The capture of a city that lies outside the boundaries of our territory is useless, and the shedding of Texan blood in such unprofitable warfare is a mistake.... Since our military power is weak, let our strength be in unity! Then we shall show our foes what a nation can do when all its citizens rise to protect their rights and say unfalteringly, "We will be free!" Let us teach these Mexicans that when a nation fights for a just cause, the Almighty Himself bears their standard.

Captain Pearson, one of the Greys' artillery officers, speaks after General Houston, saying that Santa Anna could not come before late spring and that the time to move is now. The debate goes on until late that evening, when Dr. Grant, Captain Pearson, Major Morris, and Colonel Johnson decide to depart for San Patricio the next day, from which point they will march south. Only 200 men join them. The rest are convinced that General Houston is right—Texas needs its soldiers on its own soil. They march north to Goliad.

If you decide to go with Grant,
turn to page 37

If you decide to go to Goliad,
turn to page 179

The next day, the army is on the march. After crossing the Colorado, follow the river southeast to Beason's Crossing, where you catch the road to San Felipe de Austin. It is general knowledge that General Sesma is not far behind and that Santa Anna himself is following him. Some of the men want to fight—to hold San Felipe and stop retreating. Houston knows that he must have a few days to drill the army, so he leaves a small number of his best marksmen to hold San Felipe as if Houston has to cross the Brazos there. Then you head north up the Brazos to Groce's Ferry. For almost two weeks Houston drills the Army in the battle tactics and commands he will use—when he finds a suitable place to engage the Mexican army. Finally, on April 13, the army crosses the Brazos on the steamboat *Yellowstone* and begins preparing for the march to battle.

Go on to the next page

Houston leads the army, which has grown to almost 1,000 men, directly to Harrisburg. The men are now jubilant —you are going to fight at last and stop all this retreating. Deaf Smith appears from nowhere with news of Santa Anna's plans for troop movements. Snooping in between the Mexican armies, he captured a courier carrying detailed plans. Using this information, Houston immediately begins seeking ground that will allow him both surprise and an advantageous attack position. He marches the army across Buffalo Bayou on April 19, which in turn lures Santa Anna and Sesma across. There is a short cavalry skirmish on the twentieth, but Houston does not intend to fight until the position is perfect. On the twenty-first, just after General Cós arrives to reinforce Santa Anna with another 500 soldiers, Houston sends Deaf Smith with a few other men to burn Vince's bridge, thus cutting off any easy retreat for either army. As Travis put it, "Victory or Death."

At 3 P.M., you find yourself in a line of riflemen almost 1,000 yards long. The line is broken in the middle by the Twin Sisters, two brand-new cannon, a gift from the city of Cincinnati, Ohio, to the Texas cause. Floating on a slight breeze over the cannon is a plain white flag with a long azure star in the middle. On the flag is written *Ubi Libertas Habitat, Ibi Nostra Patria Est,* Latin for "Where Liberty lives, there is our native land." The long line of infantry is flanked on the right by the cavalry—sixty of the best horsemen in Texas under Mirabeau Buonaparte Lamar. A slight rise in the open field before you hides the Texans from the Mexican camp.

Captain Juan Seguín, whose company of Tejanos served along with Deaf Smith as the army's rear guard for much of the retreat (and fought a number of skirmishes with the Mexican advance guards), refuses to be left out of the conflict. As brave as he is handsome, Seguín tells Houston that there are a number of his friends among the Alamo dead, and he will revenge them this day. Houston, who assigned the Tejanos to the rear again, fears that they might be mistaken for Mexicans during the conflict. "General Sam," says Seguín, "there are no Tejano *vaqueros* in the Mexican camp. If you catch me wearing a Mexican uniform, shoot me." Sequín and his men join Lamar's cavalry.

Incredibly, Santa Anna has become so used to chasing the Texas Army rather than fighting it that he and his army are enjoying an afternoon siesta while the battle line forms. They are located in a small wood that backs onto a swamp on one side and the waters of San Jacinto Bay and McCormick's Lake on the other. There is a mere 900 yards between the armies.

When all is ready, you look down the line to see Houston draw his sword and say a few words. You cannot hear much of what he says until he cries, "Remember the Alamo! Remember Goliad!" All at once the line surges forward. Moving up the small hill, you do remember the Alamo and Goliad—and the brave company of the New Orleans Greys. How many of them are dead, how many prisoners? How many will wear the wounds of this war like badges of honor for the rest of their lives? So much blood has been spilled already. You are very angry when you top the rise between the camps.

Close by, the Twin Sisters have been dragged along to a point where they can open up on the Mexican camp. You hear the dull thuds of the Mexican sentries' *escopetas,* followed by the roar of the Texas cannon and the sharp crack of your own rifle. Less than thirty yards now. You are running down the incline toward the Mex-

ican camp. You can see their muskets still stacked, men scrambling out of sleep—you hear a belated bugle begin to sound the alert, and the boom of Santa Anna's big cannon, the Golden Standard. Fired in fear, it is aimed far too high, sending the grapeshot over your head. Then you are on them. "Remember the Alamo! Remember Goliad!" you scream until your throat is hoarse. "Remember the Greys!" You are aware of the terror you inspire.

Somewhere you hear a drum and fife playing "Come to My Bower," the melody punctuated by gunshots and screams. The Texans pour through the camp. After three or four shots, you begin using your rifle as a club, bring it crashing down on the heads of these pour souls. "Me no Alamo!" many scream. Others fight just as fiercely as the Texans, but individually, for there is no time for the orderly tactics of battle. There is no time to form lines or columns or reload or fix bayonets. Bowie knives flash until reddened, tomahawks splinter skulls, pistols are used at point-blank range.

There is no mercy shown during the battle—which only lasts a few minutes. There is little mercy shown during the terrible rout that follows. The Mexicans are driven into the bayou, where a slaughter even greater than that of the battle occurs as Texas rifles continue to blaze away.

The following day, 630 Mexican dead are counted—about the same number of men who fell defending the Alamo and were murdered at Goliad. There are over 700 prisoners, including Santa Anna himself and most of his major officers. Of the Texans at San Jacinto, only 2 are dead, and some 30 are wounded.

Overjoyed with the victory at first, over the next few days you reflect upon the number of lives it has cost and upon the meaning of the victory gained.

"What's eating you, Tom?" asks a familiar voice one evening.

You look up to see Herman. "You're alive," you shout.

"Indeed I am," he says. "Glad I can say the same of you."

"Do you know if any other of the Greys are left?"

"None I know of. I suppose just you and me are left to tell the tale."

"Not me," you say. "Telling tales is your business. After all this death, I've got some living to do—but remember me in your book."

The Mexican response is immediate. Bugles sound and sentries call into the night. The roll of drums mingles with the wind and the deep thunder of the Alamo cannon answering those of Colonel Neill.

You are in Milam's battalion, and your lieutenant is a young Tejano of Bowie's *leoncitos* who seems to know the countryside and the habits of the Mexican forces very well. Finally some small red rockets are fired up over the walls of the Alamo. *"Mira, muchachos!"* he says to the group. "Those bright rockets are to call the troops out from the plazas of the city to reinforce the Alamo. We can attack now."

General Cós has his men quartered throughout the city, with concentrations in the larger family homes on Main Plaza and Military Plaza and in the Alamo itself. As soon as the Mexicans realize that there are Texans in the streets, the battle gets very nasty. Every window on every street the rooftop of every house, every tree, rain barrel, and shadow — all might shelter a desperate Mexican soldier. It is a cat-and-mouse battle, with a great deal of waiting and sniping.

Moving quickly down the street that first morning, the battalion secures two major homes that were commandeered by the Mexican forces, the houses of the Veramendi and de la Garza familes. For the next three days you fight house to house. Some of the men, led by Greenberry Logan and Hendrick Arnold, two freed slaves who look to you like young giants, literally move *through* the houses, breaking down walls and doors with battering rams and axes, going from one room to the next, one house to the next. But mostly it is a battle of sniping. In the dark you wait as quietly as possible until you see a Mexican rifle fire. Before the glow dies, you aim and fire and move. The Mexicans use the same trick; the moment after you fire, the place you were standing is likely to suffer a hail of return fire. In the daylight you fight just as you hunt—quietly, remaining very still, out of sight, then carefully aiming and shooting the quarry. It is so much like hunting that the fact you are killing *men* does not really hit you until you advance to the plazas, which are littered with the dead.

Most of the Mexicans are indeed armed with cast-off British smooth-bore muskets, but a few have more accurate weapons. No place is safe. On the afternoon of December 7 you return to the temporary headquarters in the Veramendi house to resupply yourself with powder and shot. In the courtyard Milam and some others are studying a map. A shot rings out from someplace high and to the east. Old Ben Milam falls dead, without even a dying word, a bullet hole in his forehead.

"Look there!" someone cries, pointing to a large cypress tree about 100 yards away. Every rifle in the courtyard is immediately trained upon the tree. A slight movement gives away the position of the sniper. A dozen guns bark, and a moment later the body of a Mexican soldier falls from the tree to the river below.

By this time, Cós's forces have mostly made their way into the Alamo. Cós now turns his cannon on the town itself, raking the streets with grapeshot and leveling houses with his nine- and twelve-pounders. Day and night the air is filled with the sharp crack of Kentucky rifles, the duller thudding of the Mexican *escopetas* (the old British muskets), the bark of your six-pounders, the woof of the middle-weight cannon, and the deep boom of the Alamo's eighteen-pounder. You lose track of Herman for an entire day, but he rejoins you at dawn on the morning of December 9. You find yourself on the eastern end of town, watching the

sunrise color the clouds above the Alamo. By the time the sun has completely risen, General Cós and his remaining forces have surrendered.

Turn to page 187

Reunited at Goliad with Herman and the remaining Greys, you hear horrifying reports. General Urrea's attack on San Patricio was indeed a massacre. Only Colonel Johnson and four others escaped to Goliad. Dr. Grant, Major Morris, and most of their men were wiped out while catching horses. The first few survivors who straggle in tell how Grant (who, as it turns out, was *hated* by the citizens of northern Mexico) was slashed to ribbons by Mexican swords. Later accounts say that Grant did not die immediately but was carried back to San Patricio, where some junior officers, after Urrea's departure, tied Grant's feet to the hind legs of a wild mustang and whipped it out of town. There was not enough of the "beloved Scot" left to bury.

The Presidio la Bahía near Goliad stands atop a hill on the southwest bank of the Río San Antonio. Ten-foot high, three-foot thick stone walls enclose a compound of a little over three acres. Inside the compound, the mission church of Espíritu Santo faces a small courtyard in the northeast corner. Unlike the Alamo, which was designed more as a mission than as a fort, La Bahía was built by Spanish soldiers as a fort to protect a mission. Fannin is determined that this is the place to make a stand—not in the already battle-pounded ruin in Béxar.

You, Herman, and the rest of the Greys, however, are worried about your friends who stayed in Béxar and request that Fannin provision the Greys to return to the Alamo. Fannin promises that supplies are on the way and that you can leave once the fort is supplied. Meanwhile, you spend your time working on a covered path down to the river (so that the fort will have water), rebuilding old bastions and constructing a new blockhouse, and burning the fields and woods all around the fort. Fannin renames the place Fort Defiance.

Captain Juan Seguín rides in from the Alamo, demanding that Fannin come to the relief of the small band besieged by Santa Anna. Fannin refuses. Even with the 500 men now in Fort Defiance, he says, they would be cut down by Santa Anna's cavalry before they ever got to Béxar. Besides, General Urrea is sure to attack Defiance any day. Seguín is sent on as a messenger to Gonzales. The Greys are united in their opinion that they will leave on their own if Fannin does not march. Finally, on February 26, Fannin orders the march to San Antonio. It only lasts one day. As well repaired as Fort Defiance is, the old ox carts used to carry the army's supplies are falling apart before the first day is past. The next morning the oxen have disappeared. Fannin gives up and orders the army back to the fort. There are no words to describe how you feel. You are sure that every step you take back to Fort Defiance is deadly to the men in Béxar.

Back at the fort, James Bonham suddenly arrives from the Alamo, his dun horse sweat-lathered and its rider looking paler than death. "Come, now, you—!" he curses at Fannin. "One hundred and eighty-two lives will be on your head as surely as if you murdered them every one." Fannin tries to convince Bonham to stay at Goliad, but the boyhood friend of William Barret Travis has only scorn for the idea. Bonham rides out of the fort loudly cursing Fannin.

It is not long afterward that you receive the news that the Alamo has fallen. Santa Anna left no defenders alive, took no prisoners. Now he is moving east. More than 500 men have gathered in Goliad under Fannin when General Houston sends orders for Fannin to abandon Goliad and bring his men north to join the rest of the army. Finally things begin to happen. Fannin sends 100 men under

Captain King and Captain Ward to help evacuate Refugio while the main force prepares to march. On March 16 a scout reports that the force under King and Ward has been wiped out by General Urrea, who is now only a few miles away. Two days later there is a small skirmish with General Urrea's advance guards. On March 19 Fannin finally gives the order to march north.

Once again, Fannin is ill-prepared for a major movement of his troops. The carts break down and the animals, overburdened by the weight of the guns they pull, weaken after only a few miles. Fannin orders a halt in the middle of a small plain, though several officers urge him to continue on to Coleto Creek, just a mile or so further. Suddenly there are Mexican soldiers on two sides of the plain, then on a third. Fannin orders a hollow square battle formation. The Greys, the Red Rovers, and a company of Kentuckians form the front line of rifleman.

General Urrea's cavalrymen attack three times, and you repulse them three times. Again you are thankful for the superior range and accuracy of your Kentucky long rifle. The Mexicans, with the *escopetas,* can hardly get close enough to fire their weapons when the Texans cut them down. There is a good deal of cheering when the cavalry attacks are repulsed, but by mid-afternoon things are pretty miserable—the sun is bearing down and you wish again that Fannin had not halted until he got to Coleto Creek with its cool water and shade trees. Hemmed in on all sides, Fannin orders you to dig trenches all night. There is no water to bathe the wounded, and their cries are pitiful. Henry Curtman, the young German who fought beside you at the Siege of Béxar, lies dead.

When the sun comes up, it reveals two shiny brass Mexican cannon. It is clear after a few minutes that the cannon will rip you all to shreds. There is no option but surrender. Within a few hours you are trudging back to Goliad—to Fort Defiance —as a prisoner of war. Some defiance, you think.

General Urrea assures Fannin and the Texas officers that you will be held as prisoners—and that the Mexican government does not execute its prisoners. Then on the morning of Palm Sunday, March 27, a Mexican officer announces that you are to be shipped back to New Orleans. The 400 survivors of the Battle of Coleto are divided into three columns and marched out of the fort. The common infantry soldiers who have guarded you this past week are sullen, silent, speaking only to order you to move along. You find this odd, since you are being marched to freedom. "Sour grapes," says Herman, who is just ahead of you in line. Peter Mattern, just ahead of Herman, shushes you both and says, "Look, the guards are filing off to the side."

Up ahead someone cries out, "No hope is left! The last hour of the Greys has come! Comrades . . . !" The voice is cut off by a rifle volley. "Run!" shouts Herman. There is nothing but gun smoke and silence for a moment. Peter Mattern lies at your feet with a portion of his skull blown

away. Then you hear the command to reload being shouted. You run. The screams of the wounded are drowned by another roar from the line of rifles. A bullet passes through your left arm—something you notice almost as if it were someone else. Your entire mind is bent on running, getting to the Río San Antonio, following Herman, who keeps calling "Run, Tom! Run!"

A Mexican soldier appears out of nowhere, sword in hand, but Herman simply runs him down. You both fling yourselves into the river—where you find that your wounded arm suddenly will not work. Flailing with one arm, with bullets ripping the water all around you, somehow you reach the other shore. Hidden in the undergrowth, Herman bandages your arm. It is only a flesh wound but is beginning to hurt terribly. Turning to Herman, who is himself nursing a sword cut, you say, "I think it's about time we joined up with old Houston."

Under the cover of darkness that night, you begin a slow and painful journey north.

Turn to page 119

After Cós surrenders, General Burleson obtains his personal parole—his word of honor as a soldier and a gentleman—that the Mexican general will accompany his 1,105 troops south of the Río Grande and that neither he nor his officers will "in any way oppose the reestablishment of the Federal Constitution of 1824." As one Mexican officer puts it when he signs the agreement, "All has been lost save honor."

It is a glorious moment indeed—no more than 300 Texans have whipped the cream of the Mexican army. Casualties on the Mexican side are five times that of the Texans' twenty-eight dead and wounded. Too glorious, perhaps, for the Texas volunteers begin packing up and leaving as soon as the Mexican army is out of sight. They have families and farms to attend to, and no one thinks that Mexican troops will set foot again on Texas soil until late next spring. Even General Burleson heads for his home, leaving Béxar under the command of Colonel Frank Johnson. "It's not over, for sure," says Herman Ehrenberg, "but there is not going to be much to do until it fires up again."

That is not exactly true. The inhabitants of San Antonio de Béxar turn out to be just as ardent supporters of the cause of liberty as the army itself. A party begins that will last through Christmas and into January. It is a delightful time. Before Christmas, there are Posada processions through the streets, reenacting the Holy Family's search for shelter so long ago. After Christmas there is a very strange play put on about the shepherds of Bethlehem who must fight their way past oddly costumed devils to get to the manger. Every night there is excellent singing in the cathedral of San Fernando. On the other hand, every night there is excellent singing, dancing, flirting, and drinking in the little town's three cantinas—where Herman at last gets to play the part of a liberating soldier.

But the Greys and other volunteers came to Texas to fight—not to romance the señoritas and drink rum. Dr. James Grant, a Scot with a gift for inspiring glorious military dreams, argues day and night with anyone who will listen that the thing to do is to take the war to Mexico. "Only a great fool would think that old devil Santa Anna is going to sit still when we've insulted him by driving all his fine and fancy troops out of Texas. We hold the fortress of Béxar and we hold Presidio la Bahía at Goliad. Why wait for Santa Anna to march into Texas with who knows how large an army? Or with more than one army? The thing to do is to attack the Mexicans on their own soil. We've got to march on Matamoros! It is a rich city and there will be plenty of the spoils of war to be had for the taking!"

With such rousing speeches and enticing promises Dr. Grant inspires the men. James Fannin, Bowie's co-commander at the Battle of Concepción, is already gathering volunteers at Copano on the coast, and is ready to march south. Colonel Frank Johnson, now in command of the forces at Béxar, agrees with Grant, and together they plan an expedition to Matamoros, 300 miles to the south near the mouth of the Río Grande. Jim Bowie and Colonel Neill argue that the men are thinking more about the silver mines of Matamoros than of the military needs of Texas. It is December 30—Dr. Grant is leaving tonight. Already some 200 men have agreed to go on the expedition to Matamoros, including Henry, Peter, and Herman, along with most the Greys.

190

*If you decide to go with Dr. Grant,
turn to page 159*

*If you decide to stay in Bexar,
go on to the next page*

By mid-January things in San Antonio de Béxar have slowed to a standstill. You have taken up quarters in the Alamo barracks. The garrison has dwindled to a mere 100 men, mostly volunteers from the southern states, under the command of Colonel J. C. Neill and Jim Bowie. Most of the volunteers are either hunters and trappers or professional men —lawyers, doctors, businessmen, and a few career soldiers. A few wives and children stay in Béxar. There are very few farmers among this crew.

General Houston ordered Bowie to blow up the Alamo, if Bowie thought it could not be defended, and to move the troops to Gonzales, where Houston can train them with the rest of the Texas Army quartered there. Finally, on February 2, Bowie writes a letter to Governor Smith, who is currently in charge of what government there is in Texas:

> *The salvation of Texas depends in great measure on keeping Béxar out of the hands of the enemy. It stands on the frontier picquet guard, and if it was in the possession of Santa Anna, there is no stronghold from which to repel him in his*

*march to the Sabine. Colonel
Neill and myself have come to
the solemn resolution that we
will rather die in these ditches
than give it up to the enemy.*

You have to admit that there is not
much to hold Béxar with, should the Mexican army invade Texas again. When Dr.
Grant left, he and the Matamoros expedition took most of the food, medicine, and
just about every gun in the place. Jim
Bowie, whose reputation as a knife-fighter
has made him into a living legend, has organized the children to gather cannonballs remaining among the debris in
Béxar itself, but the Alamo cannon still
lack powder. The fort itself has taken
quite a pounding—you regret now having
been so carefree about the number of
cannonballs you lobbed at it, but then
you never thought that you might have to
defend the place anytime soon. Rumors
are already circulating that Santa Anna is
on his way, and this time he is bringing
thousands of troops.

Gradually, men begin to drift into San
Antonio as the rumors spread—men who
also believe that it is important to hold
Béxar. As one Texan put it who was
returning after spending Christmas with

his family, "I shore would hate for that cussed old Santa Anna to walk right into this place when I done worked so hard to take it away from Señor Cós." Green B. Jameson, a mechanically minded lawyer, has become the Alamo "engineer," putting just about everybody to work with shovels and axes and saws. Bowie's local Tejano friends begin stocking the Alamo corral with a remuda of fine horses for long-range scouting.

In early February a red-headed lawyer, Lieutenant Colonel William Barret Travis, arrives at the Alamo with thirty men. A week later, none other than Davy Crockett saunters into town, bringing with him a dozen Tennesseans and some other volunteers picked up along the way. Since the few Greys left in the Alamo are claiming no one in particular as their captain, you adopt the legendary bear hunting, Indian fighting, Congressifying Crockett as your captain. He doesn't mind at all.

Turn to page 76

When you arrive back in Gonzales on March 11, the first thing you hear is that the Alamo has fallen. Every single defender was put to the sword, just as the bloodred banner flying from the San Fernando bell tower promised. The only Alamo survivors were a few women and children, mostly Tejanos native to San Antonio. Only three Americans survived—Mrs. Dickinson, her daughter Angelina, and Travis's slave Joe, who have just arrived in Gonzales under the escort of Houston's chief scout, Deaf Smith. You know that there were other Anglo children in the Alamo who must have been killed, like the two sons of the Englishman Antony Wolfe, who were only a year or two younger than you. But the defenders performed brilliantly—670 out of 800 of Santa Anna's best shock troop died. In all, almost 2,000 Mexican soldiers remained in Béxar, 1,600 of them permanently. At first you want to cry, but that emotion is replaced almost at once by a cold fury. You feel a deep sense of shame, even though you were ordered out as a messenger, that you were not there to fight and die beside such brave men. You vow that you will take revenge.

The next two weeks are filled with stop-and-go marches. Houston orders several

men in the army to act as Rangers, helping the settlers who have suddenly filled
every road leading away from Santa
Anna. Most of the citizens of Béxar have
slipped into the countryside to hide, but
the people of Gonzales and Bastrop and
from all the little farms and *ranchos* in
this part of the country are fleeing. They
have left their houses and stores open and
turned loose their stock. Already the
Rangers have shot a few looters. Although
people are calling this the "Runaway
Scrape," the army moves at anything but

a run. Finally, on March 17, you reach
Burnham's Crossing on the Colorado
River.

Turn to page 163

FURTHER READING

In and out of school, it has been my experience that *real* history is much more interesting than textbook history, and that accurate historical fiction is even better. Here are a few favorites.

For Younger Readers

The Boy in the Alamo by Margaret Cousins (Corona Publishing). This delightful novel tells the story of how 12-year-old Billy Campbell followed his brother Buck and Davy Crockett to the Alamo.

James Butler Bonham: Rebel Hero by Jean Flynn (Eakin Press). A brief and lively account of Bonham's life that tells a lot about the kind of men who found their way into the fight for liberty in Texas.

Make Way for Sam Houston by Jean Fritz (Putnam Publishing). An accurate and appealing biography of the man the Cherokees knew as "Big Drunk" and the Texas Army as "the Old General."

200

For Older Readers

Rendezvous at the Alamo by Virgil E. Baugh (University of Nebraska Press). Brief biographical summaries of the lives of Bowie, Crockett, and Travis.

Lone Star: A History of Texas and Texans by T. R. Fehrenbach (Macmillan Publishing). The best history of the state available.

Reminiscences of Fifty Years in Texas by John Linn (State House Books). Linn was an Irishman who arrived in Texas as a colonist in 1829. He fought in the Battle of Gonzales and at San Jacinto. Later he was an important political figure in the Republic. His reminiscences form one of the most important sources we have on the Texas Revolution.

A Time to Stand by Walter Lord (Pocket Books). Still the best of the many books dealing specifically with the Battle of the Alamo—a subject that remains rife with conflicting numbers, dates, and opinions. Lord's book is highly readable as well.

Viva Tejas: The Story of the Tejanos, the Mexican Born Patriots of the Texas

Revolution by Ruben Rendon Lozano, edited by Mary Ann Noonan Guerra (Alamo Press). One of the very few reliable sources on the Tejanos active in the Texas Revolution.

A Historical Atlas of Texas by William C. Pool, maps by Edward Triggs and Lance Wren (Encino Press). The best source on the subject.

The Evolution of a State, or Recollections of Old Texas Days by Noah Smithwick (University of Texas Press). J. Frank Dobie called this the "best of all books dealing with life in early Texas." It is hard to disagree. Smithwick participated in the Battle of Gonzales and the Battle of Concepción and was the first Texas blacksmith to make a Bowie knife for Jim Bowie. Later he served with the Texas Rangers. This is an excellent book to catch the flavor and harsh reality of life in early Texas.